D0936430

THE ADVENTURES OF CAPTAIN ALONSO de CONTRERAS

THE ADVENTURES OF CAPTAIN ALONSO de CONTRERAS

† A 17TH CENTURY JOURNEY †

TRANSLATED AND ANNOTATED BY

Philip Dallas

PARAGON HOUSE

New York

First edition, 1989

Published in the United States by
Paragon House
90 Fifth Avenue
New York, NY 10011

Copyright © 1989 by Paragon House

Manufactured in the United States of America

Library of Congress Cataloging-in-Publication Data

Contreras, Alonso de, b. 1582.
[Vida de] capitán Contreras. English]
The adventures of Captain Alonso de Contreras : a 17th century journey /
translated and annotated by Philip Dallas. — 1st ed.
p. cm.
Translation of: Vida del capitán Contreras.
ISBN 1-55778-168-0 : $19.95
1. Contreras, Alonso de, b. 1582—Diaries.   2. Soldiers—Spain—Diaries.
I. Dallas, Philip.   II. Title.
DP183.9.C6A3
946'.051'092—dc20
[B]   89-32654
                                                CIP

The paper used in this publication meets the minimum requirements of
American National Standard for Information Sciences—Permanence of Paper
for Printed Library Materials, ANSI Z39.48-1984.

The original Spanish text of Contreras's autobiography was 'lost' for three centuries and then published in the Boletino d'Istoria of Madrid in the late 19th century; a copy of which is available in the British Museum.

The underlined part of the text is an annotation to facilitate the reader in understanding the historical context which Contreras at times did not fully understand.

This is not a novel but a fairly accurate historical document and recognized as such by historians.

CONTENTS

Chapter Eleven

Chapter Twelve

Chapter Thirteen

Chapter Fourteen

Chapter Fifteen

Chapter Sixteen

INTRODUCTION

In the year 1600, Alonso de Contreras was eighteen and already a professional soldier—a Spanish Rambo, a mercenary—who joined any expedition, irrespective of the danger, to fight the Turks and earn the prize money. At the same time, the English were founding the State of Virginia. This was a time when the power structure of the Western World was tilting in favor of the northern countries at the expense of the Mediterranean lands that had previously held the power.

The Turks, too, were always ready for a fight, but, like the Spaniards, they were beginning to feel the great shift in power. The Mediterranean was becoming a backwater, while the Atlantic and even the Indian Ocean were becoming the essence of the future. The papacy, despite its fabulous swan song of Berninian architecture and sculpture that impressed the world, was being superseded by the new Protestant powers of England, Germany, the Netherlands, and, to a lesser extent, France, which were not only taking political and military power but also world trade into their hands. However, they did little to protect Europe from the Turks, who were the foremost enemy of southeastern Europe, having extended their empire as far as Greece and Vienna and down the whole coast of Palestine to Egypt, Libya, Algeria and, finally, Spain, which had repulsed them. The task of containing and maiming the Turks (and, for that matter, saving the rest of Europe from conquest by them) and their Arab allies was carried out by the Spaniards and their most distinguished allies, the knights of Malta.

These violent days have been recorded in our history books and one can reasonably ask what Alonso de Contreras can add to conventional wisdom and knowledge about them. The answer to this is that the tales Contreras has to tell record not only highly personal vicissitudes but also depict a colorful life that might well be considered unique. Some who have read the Spanish text call it fanciful; others (including the authoritative historian Huizinga) credit it as veracious. Whichever view is correct, the life of Captain Alonso de Contreras, knight of Malta, makes entertaining reading as well as showing new facets of the philosophy, ethics, morality, and lifestyle of those times.

Contreras recounted his life, but he did not write a history book, for the good reasons that he did not always know what was going on (and probably cared less) and, in any case, history is, of necessity, hindsight, whereas his text was written while he was still using his sword and pistols.

This, then, leaves me the task of filling in many lacunae—the wheres, the whys, and the whos—as well as a general background on the Order of Malta, the Spanish Empire and much else. I, therefore, must ask the reader to bear with me as I paint a picture of the power structures in which Contreras played his part. This will give the reader the opportunity to better understand Contreras's private and public life.

Alonso de Contreras was not only a unique Rambo in his actions; he was also a unique member of the aristocratic military and religious Order of Malta. He was the only plebeian ever to be admitted to the Order, and then only because he had been made a knight by a pope—Pope Urban VIII, who was the pope who set

Bernini to rebuild papal Rome with the statues, palaces, fountains, and churches that still delight and impress us. This great Barberini pope made Contreras a knight for his derring-do and his war against the enemies of Christendom. Such was his reputation that, throughout many ports of the Mediterranean, his portrait was hung, cowboy-style, under a "Wanted by the Turks, Good Bounty Paid" offer.

Contreras was "wanted" by the police at the age of fourteen while still a schoolboy. He knifed a school companion who told on him for playing hooky, which got him a thrashing from his schoolmaster. He was tried and sent for a year into "exile" from Madrid in the custody of an uncle who was the rector of a church: This rector must have given young Alonso a good education during that year as, throughout his life, he demonstrated not only a broad catholic culture but a scientific turn of mind in becoming a sea captain, Atlantic Ocean navigator, and mapmaker.

Contreras was far from being of noble blood: His parents were poor but not destitute. After his exile, his widowed mother wanted him to become a silversmith, but this sedentary profession did not fit his dreams of glory. He began his autobiography: "I was born in that most noble city of Madrid on 6 January 1582." At the age of fifteen, he left that noble city as a camp follower of an army marching to the Spanish Netherlands.

He started writing his story in Palermo at fifty years of age, waiting for a ship to take him to Malta. He had quarreled with the Spanish viceroys of both Naples and Sicily and had time on his hands. Many years before, experiencing difficulties of career and money and waiting for a new command in Madrid, Contreras had been a houseguest of the famous Spanish playwright Lope de Vega for eight months. Lope de Vega was also a Knight of Malta, which explains the link between this tough soldier of fortune and the elegant writer, twenty years his senior. The former must have entertained the latter with the stories of his life and been encouraged to put them down on paper, which he did many years later, though the manuscripts vanished into the Madrid archives for centuries before they were published in the *State Historical Bulletin* rather than in book form.

Contreras wrote his life story beginning with his childhood. He covered sheets of paper with anecdotes, vaguely in the order in which they happened. He apparently did not care how unfavorable a picture they gave of himself, and this, in itself, persuades one to conclude that he wrote the truth because he scarcely had even the time to invent lies: He wrote most of this manuscript in only eleven days.

Despite how little he knew about writing books, Contreras could not have written a better opening sentence: It sums up the two most important factors in his extraordinary life. One, Contreras was a Spaniard and proud of it, and, two, he was born in the middle of one of the most full-blooded, violent, and active periods of Europe's history.

In 1582, the year of Contreras's birth, the Spanish Empire had stretched its frontiers to California, Mexico, Peru, and even to the Philippine Islands. In Europe, Spanish rule reached the Netherlands, Burgundy, Milan, as well as southern Italy, Sardinia, and Sicily. Spanish arms and priests were spreading the Christian religion throughout the New World and, at the same time, defending Europe from the infidel Turk and Moor. It was the peak of Spanish glory.

During this period, the summit of Spanish art was reached. Cervantes wrote *Don Quixote,* while Lope de Vega penned his hundreds of plays. As for painting, Velázquez, Zurbarán and Murillo's work was more than a continuation of the Italian tradition: It was the essence and spirit of Spain. The artists' subjects ranged from scintillating kings and sombre monks at prayer to peasant boys pensively eating grapes. Alonso de Contreras had good reason, then, to be proud to be a Spaniard, but his pride was not of the sort that hastens to hide faults, failures, or a humble start in life.

Although he spent time in Sicily, Naples, Rome, Spain, the

Caribbean, and the Netherlands, most of Contreras's time was divided between Malta and the coastline of the Mediterranean. The background of the knights of Malta and the Turks—the major protagonists of Contreras's life—is therefore important.

The Turks built a great empire that lasted a thousand years and was finally destroyed only in World War I, when its territories (Syria, Iraq, Iran, Saudi Arabia, the Yemen, Egypt, Libya, Algeria, and Morocco, among others) were divided up between English, French, and Spanish spheres of interest. In all events, at the time of Contreras, the Turks were not at their strongest: They had lost out heavily at the Siege of Malta and at the sea battle of Lepanto at the hands of Spain, the Order of Malta, the Venetian Republic, and the papacy.

What follows is a thumbnail story of the remarkable Turks, who, with their extreme bellicosity, probably did more to wear down the strength of Spain than any other group.

The Turks had a rapid rise to power from their most modest beginnings. In the year 1300, Othman, a native of Asia Minor (Turkey), founded a tribe of warlike goatherds who soon expanded at such speed that they were making attacks on the dying Byzantine (East Roman) Empire. Within fifty years of their foundation, these goatherds, soon to be known as the Ottomans, were a considerable power and had established their capital at Brusa. Although still warlike, they were also cautious. Indeed, their preference for consolidating a smaller area and administrating it well rather than poorly controlling a large rambling empire would continue to be a primary Turkish characteristic for centuries to come. Acting on this policy, Orchan, Othman's eldest son, organized his new state and built hospitals, schools, military establishments, and mosques.

At this time, Orchan also instituted his military elite, the janissaries. During his attacks on the Byzantine Empire, he captured large numbers of Greek boys, the healthiest of whom he put under strict discipline and trained as soldiers. This institution continued for centuries, and new generations of Greek lads were the support of the Turkish Empire not only in the army but also in the administration. During the second half of the fourteenth century, the Ottomans started crossing the Dardanelles into Europe. Despite the federation of all the Eastern European countries (even the Mongols joined the federation to keep the Turks out), the Ottomans forged onward to the Danube. With the turn of the century, the Turks experienced success on one hand and disaster on the other. They gave the Greek emperor orders to leave Constantinople, but Tamerlane (the Mongol) swept down on Asia Minor with his barbarian army, looted the Ottoman Empire, and carried the sultan off to Samarkand.

The vacillating Greek emperor in Constantinople made no effort to exploit the misfortunes of the Turks and even left them with their new capital at Adrianople on the European mainland. The next fifty years saw the rebuilding of the Turkish forces and the capture of Constantinople, despite the defense by the combined forces of Christendom under the Hungarian John Hunyadi.

The Ottomans continued to score military and naval successes. They took Dalmatia (Yugoslavia), Lemnos, and Morea from the Venetian Republic, thus staking their claim on the Greek peninsula. After 1512, Sultan Salim I conquered Syria, Egypt, and Arabia. Soliman the Magnificent took Rhodes from the knights of St. John (later to be called the knights of Malta) and Belgrade from the Hungarians. The loss of these two bastions was a severe shock to Europe, because both were buffer states between infidel and Christian states, and both the Hungarians and the knights had fine military reputations.

However, the next Turkish effort, the seizing of Malta in 1565, failed disastrously. Six years later, the Turks were soundly beaten at sea by the fleet of Don John of Austria at Lepanto. After that, the Turkish Empire was in a state of disruption for many years. It was only at the time that this autobiography of Contreras was written that Murad IV crushed all opposition and reestablished the empire.

During the greater part of the seventeenth century, the Turks held much of Hungary and Transylvania. They captured Crete from the Venetians in 1669. They fought the Russians for control of the Ukraine, and they invaded Austria. But, in this last effort, they were defeated by the brilliant action of the veteran Polish general Sobieski at Vienna in 1699. After that third sound defeat, the Turks were forced back into the Balkans, never again to menace Christian Europe.

This unending war between Islam and Christendom went on over the centuries, often with decades of calm, often with major land and sea battles, though, after the crusades, the West cannot be said to have carried the war to the enemy's camp. They were on the defensive, and Contreras and men like him would spy on the movements of the Turkish fleet to find out whether they would be making an attack on any Western port town, in which case the fleets of Spain and the knights of Malta would be readied.

When the fifteen-year-old Alonso decided on a life of adventure and joined the baggage train of an army leaving Madrid, as far as he was concerned it was for a destination unknown and one never reached. The destination, however, was Flanders, the Catholic province of the Netherlands that had been attacked by the English Earl of Leicester under Queen Elizabeth and then by the French under Henry IV, who had captured the towns of Picardy and Amiens. The rather meandering route the Spanish prince cardinal, commander of this army, took to Flanders can be explained by the fact that Spain had a corridor of land running from Savona (near Genoa) to Milan and through Franche

Compte (Burgundy) to Flanders (Belgium)—a most curious route, as curious as Spanish dominion over Belgium. However, due to obscure treaty conditions, the Spaniards lost all this territory in 1620.

Already, in this period, Spain had begun to find itself faced by a new world power, England. The most important encounter was the sea battle in which the Spanish fleet, the Armada of stately Spanish galleons, was in 1588 badly mauled by the swift little frigates of the English.

This David and Goliath battle continued over the decades and extended its ground to the other side of the Atlantic, where Sir Walter Raleigh and his colleagues used to capture Spanish galleons loaded with gold on their way home from Peru and Mexico: Some of this gold is still on the ceiling of the Consistory Hall in the Vatican, and it is said by economists that the looted gold formed the capital base for the military-industrial take-off of English economic power. Contreras encountered Sir Walter Raleigh's little fleet in the Caribbean, as it was dispersing before returning home after a failed project to found a settlement on the Orinoco River in northern Brazil. Contreras succeeded in capturing one of the five English ships, but the others, after a few exchanges of cannonballs, slipped through Contreras's fingers, as the English ships were faster and their sailors more expert at maneuvering. This battle took place off Puerto Rico. On the ship Contreras captured, he found twenty-one English sailors whom he took prisoner and disembarked at Havana, Cuba, where he had general supplies and explosives as well as reinforcements for the garrisons to put ashore.

The life of Alonso de Contreras not only spanned the Atlantic but also two distinct eras of history: the former that of the old Mediterranean world and the latter the vast opening of horizons in the New World. He was also, for the record, embarked at one stage in his life, with a battalion of infantry on galleons destined for the Philippines, but because orders were changed he did not get to see Spain's most distant outpost.

However, because his life was mostly with the Order of Malta, a brief rundown of their history will be helpful.

Between the ninth and twelfth centuries, the Republic of Amalfi flourished. As early as the year 849, the fleets of Amalfi, Naples, and Gaeta saved Rome from the Saracens (the Moors of North Africa).

The Amalfitans were great seamen. They had colonies and trading posts throughout the whole of the Mediterranean littoral. In the beginning of the eleventh century, they founded the church of Santa Maria de la Latina in Jerusalem for the use of the Amalfitan colony there. Soon after, they set up a hospice to shelter women visiting the Holy Sepulchre; it was this Santa Maria Maddalena hospice that ultimately became the home of the religious order for women affiliated to the Order of St. John of Jerusalem. As the number of pilgrims increased, the Amalfitans founded a hospital under the name of St. John the Baptist.

During and after the siege of Jerusalem in 1087, Brother Gerardo Sasso, the head of the hospital and an Amalfian, gave great assistance to the Crusaders. In gratitude, they showered the hospital with privileges and gifts of money and land. Sasso took full advantage of his popularity and made his hospital a large and important institution in Jerusalem.

Some twenty years after the siege, Brother Gerardo changed the rule of the hospital from that of St. Benedict to that of St. Augustine and designed a black habit with a white cross on the breast for the brothers to wear.

It should be remembered that, at that time, all monasteries were quite independent of each other. The fact that they followed the spiritual rule of St. Benedict or St. Augustine did not put them under the discipline of any high authority in Italy in the way that the master general of the Dominican Order later controlled, and still controls, all Dominicans throughout the world. However, Brother Gerardo's new establishment, having received the sanction of Pope Pascal II, was taken directly under the private care of the papacy. Pope Pascal's act was confirmed by Pope Calixtus II in 1119 and by many later popes. So, in this way, the history and privileges of the knights were founded.

Raymond de Puy became master of the order on the death of Brother Gerardo Sasso. He changed the nature of the order and, in less than twenty years, he had knights of the Order of St. John of Jerusalem fighting the Wars of the Cross in full armor.

Between the years 1120 and 1150, establishments, hospitals and a new system of commanderies were set up in the Holy Land, Western Europe, and all along the pilgrim routes. The order had been given so much property throughout Europe that a means of governing it was needed. It was, therefore, broken up into commanderies that were estates of a convenient size. They were then entrusted, in the main, to knights whose fighting days were over—a sort of pension scheme. The knight who was honored with a commandery was responsible for the managing of the estate and was able to live a comfortable retired life on its income. However, each commandery had to pay part of its income to the treasury of the order and had to send supplies of luxuries for the hospital patients. Some would send white flour, others blankets, and others linen bedsheets. If a commandery fell vacant, the year's income from the estate had to be paid to the treasury of the grand master of the order. Contreras, at the end of his fighting career, was given one of these in Spanish Leon.

Members of the "Religion" (as the Order of Malta was often called) were of three categories in those days: knights of justice, who were all of noble blood; chaplains, priests, and almoners; and brothers servants-at-arms. There are more categories today.

The statutes regulating the life of the members, including their admission, discipline and punishments, were similar to those of the Knights Templar, but, whereas the Knights Templar was a purely military and monastic organization, the Religion always remained basically a nursing brotherhood and, for that reason, its members were commonly called the Hospitalers. Throughout their history, they employed eminent physicians and surgeons to care for their patients as they still do today. The Hospitalers kept as their guiding rule that patients were to give orders and they were to obey. The Hospitalers also encouraged women to join their order as nuns, either in the active role of nursing the sick on the pilgrim routes and in the Holy Land, or in enclosed and contemplative convents in Europe. The Templars did nothing of the sort. And, it must be admitted, Alonso de Contreras makes no mention of even taking anybody's temperature.

After 178 years of flourishing, declining, fighting the Saracens, internecine warring with the Templars and the Teutonic knights, and nursing the sick, the Hospitalers, along with all the other Christians, were driven from the Holy Land by the Saracens, and the order took refuge on the isle of Cyprus.

In 1325, they moved to Rhodes, where they reestablished themselves and prospered for two hundred years. From there, they continued their hospital work, policed the seas with their-jfleet, and, through their consuls in Egypt and Jerusalem, looked after the interests of the pilgrims. Though the crusading spirit had, during this period, died in Europe, the knights kept up an active warfare with the Turks as well as trading with them—this last habit being much to the disapproval of the papacy.

The Religion, with negligible help from the rest of Europe, retarded the rise of the Ottoman Empire and, in particular, its naval power, by continuous attacks on Turkish shipping. It was in Rhodes that the Religion split up into national *langues* (languages, or tongues) each under its own prior. This was probably a protective measure taken by the Spanish and Italian knights against the Francophone knights, who had a numerical superiority in the order. It is possible that the eight-pointed cross, which became their logo, originated at that time, because the order split into eight *langues*.

In 1525, Soliman the Magnificent besieged the knights, but they succeeded in making a withdrawal from Rhodes to Crete with all the honors of war. Then, for more than five years, the knights were homeless. Many of them went from royal court to royal court in search either of employment or a means of getting the order functioning again.

King Henry VIII of England was visited by Grand Master L'Isle Adam and, at the latter's request, wrote to many of the important kings of Europe asking for help for the order to find a new home. He took a considerable part in putting the order's case before Emperor Charles V, who eventually gave the knights the islands of Malta and Gozo and the fortress of Tripoli in Libya. It should be mentioned that this gift was not made entirely out of generosity; Charles V found these three places difficult and expensive to maintain.

A short time later, when Henry VIII proclaimed himself head of the church in England—and the prior of the Hospitalers in England refused to recognize his spiritual supremacy—the king confiscated all the lands of the order within his domains and, by that act, reduced the English *langue* to poverty and finally to extinction. It was, however, much later reestablished as a Protestant, but still nursing, order.

After the fertile island of Rhodes, the treeless dry rock of Malta was not looked upon with much favor by the knights. Nevertheless, in less than thirty-five years, they had built a fine port, a town and fortifications strong enough to withstand the most famous siege in history—that of Malta in 1565, when 25,000 Turks were killed in four months before the siege ended with the arrival of Spanish reinforcements from Sicily. The battle was fought with utmost savagery: The Turks crucified captured knights and floated them across the Grand Harbor back to the fortifications of the order. The knights, in retaliation, hung their prisoners from the walls in full view of the Turks.

It can fairly be said that the Hospitalers, by their valiant defense of Malta, saved Western Europe and Italy in particular from further Turkish aggression. The knights also took a considerable part in the battle of Lepanto that took place shortly afterward, when Don John of Austria finally halted the Turks at sea, as we have noted previously. After that came the Religion's period of grandeur and the handsome city of La Valetta was built by thousands of slaves in honor of the Grand Master La Valetta, the hero of the siege.

The site of La Valetta had proved to be tactically important because the battles during the siege took place there. However, its terrain was not by any means ideal for building a city, as it sloped away steeply to the sea on either side. So, rather in the way that the palaces of the Caesars were built over arches and tunnels on the side of the Palatine Hill, Valetta was built. The miles of underground passages were used as granaries and stores for munitions and other staples.

Fine churches were built, the greatest being the co-cathedral of St. John. Each of the *langues* had a side chapel and each, it seems, vied with the others for splendor in its carvings, statuary, mosaics, and gold and silver altar pieces. The interior of St. John's is still one of the most remarkable in the world, especially when its sixteen immense Gobelin tapestries are hung. The exterior, on the other hand, is very simple and was designed in such a way that the church could be defended if need arose.

Each *langue* or national priory built also its own grand palace, or *auberge* as they were called. The Auberge of Castille is the most impressive and perfectly situated, overlooking the Grand Harbor, and its façade is carved in a handsome high baroque style from the softstone of Malta.

The finishing touch for this city was given it by the "invincible" fortifications designed by Vauban. This great French master of seventeenth-century defense designed the most impressive bastions in the world.

It was during this period, a time in which there was little fighting on any large scale, that Alonso de Contreras lived. It was a period of crowning glory but had all the seeds of decay. The Religion's wealth was immense, acquired from the income on commanderies, commerce, and the prizes of war. The order became more and more aristocratic, which makes Contreras's entrance into the order as a knight even more remarkable.

Except for some notable victories over the Turks in the early eighteenth century, the Religion was becoming ineffective and anachronistic. The knights slowly got out of touch with the spirit of Europe; in a Europe that was involved in religious wars between Protestant and Catholic and subsequently influenced by the new secular spirit of the rationalists, the knights were still faithfully keeping the Turk away from the door.

It took the French Revolution and Napoleon Bonaparte to destroy the order and capture Malta. Malta had become a refuge for the emigré royalty and nobility of France during the Revolution and so had gained the enmity of the revolutionaries and of Napoleon. The property of the Religion in French territory was confiscated in 1792, and, in 1798, Napoleon, on his way to Egypt, captured Malta.

The French knights had either become influenced by the new revolutionary spirit or realized that their order was already doomed. They treacherously opened the gates of the city and Malta was taken, despite its invincible though never tested bastions, without a shot being fired.

From that day on, the knights of Malta took no further part in the history of Europe: They modestly engaged themselves, as an Order of Chivalry retaining their sovereign rights, as a nursing brotherhood. Their present home is in the center of Rome, but at the time that Alonso Contreras took refuge aboard one of their galleys, the knights were a great power in the Mediterranean.

The knights by no means lived permanently at Malta or even in the establishments of the Religion. If they wished to keep their rights and seniority, however, they had to do a certain number of *caravans* or tours of duty with the fleet. With the rest of their time, they could look after their own estates or serve in the army or government of any Catholic country. Being a knight of St. John was a great advantage in almost every official appointment, and, over and above that, the knights had the right, if accused of any misdeed, of being judged by the prior of their own *langue*. In the first place, a knight had to be a bachelor, and, in the second, a "religious." But from parts of Contreras's story, one gathers they were often not very virtuous.

Contreras had become a non-noble member of the order, a brother servant-at-arms, in 1611, at the age of twenty-nine, in the Castille *langue* and a knight of justice at the age of forty-eight "by reason of his great prowess and fine deeds." One can, in fact, become a duly dubbed knight of Malta even today for "fine deeds," which normally include a personal contribution of service (chiefly medical service) to the order (which even maintains leper colonies in Africa) and financial support for their mobile disaster relief ambulance service rather than slitting Turkish throats.

How young Alonso got involved with the knights of Malta is a curious tale. On the road to Milan, his troop sergeant deserted and made for Naples, ordering Alonso to follow him. Only later did Contreras discover that he, too, had deserted, and he was bundled aboard a ship for Palermo. There, however, life—the military life—opened up for him. He was enrolled with a Spanish infantry company as the commander's shield and lance carrier. He even went on a raiding expedition to Patras in Greece, where he first heard the whistle of bullets and cannonballs and earned his first prize money. He was still young and inexperienced, however, and was fooled into lending his captain's best clothes and jeweled accessories to a trickster, allegedly to put on a theatrical show for the troops, who deserted and vanished during the night. Terrified of his commander's reaction, Alonso went down to the port in search of an escape route. There he found a galley of the Order of Malta that welcomed him aboard: Thus he met his destiny at an early age. The ship docked at Malta, and his new-found friends, knights of Malta aboard, quickly found Alonso a job with one of the grand master's senior aides. After a quiet year there, he returned to Palermo, where, with his old captain, he started his career of chasing Moorish corsairs and Turkish cargo ships and getting his share of the bounty, which was sometimes a hundred times his basic pay or more. It was during this long series of successful exploits that Alonso became fascinated with navigation and spent all of his time on the bridge learning about the various ports and coastlines, the depth of the water, and other such essential details.

Ashore, he was less sage. He and two other young soldiers, loaded with prize money, became known as the viceroy's Levantines—swashbuckling buccaneers who would as willingly stick a knife into you as say good morning.

Unfortunately, one of them did knife an innkeeper, and the three soldiers escaped the wrath of everybody and made for Naples, commandeering a sailing boat they found in the harbor. The viceroy of Naples ignored the gravity of their crime and enrolled them in his infantry. Then, for a second time, they were involved in a riot and had to flee from justice. Alonso's two friends were caught, but he succeeded in finding a ship of the Order of Malta, skippered by a friend who hid him till they sailed.

Alonso de Contreras was then eighteen years old, and he spent the next two years raiding the Turks, their towns, and their shipping; he describes many of these raids in lively detail. By this time, Contreras had learned what *quiraca* meant, and he had enough money to learn more. The *quiracas* of Malta were courtesans, ladies of the town, noted for their beauty and intelligence.

By this time, Contreras's fame had reached the grand master of the Order of Malta, who sent for him and promoted him to sea captain, giving him the command of a frigate and orders to search out the Turkish fleet and discover the plans of the Grand Turk (the ruler of Turkey). This was a dangerous and exciting operation in which Contreras succeeded in getting the news back to Italy that the Turks were intending to make an amphibious operation on Reggio Calabria, fighting his way through the Turkish fleet to take the news to Taormina and Malta.

Life in Malta was made up of festas, but Contreras did not always attend them, as he had a *quiraca* of his own of whom he was very jealous, to the point of not letting her be seen in public. She was displeased with this, as she enjoyed festas. On the Feast Day of St. Gregory, however, the escape of the bake-house slaves took place, when everybody had left La Valetta for the festa. Only Contreras was aware of the escape, and he manned his frigate with fishermen he shanghaied on the docks. With no inconsiderable panache, he captured the slaves as they were sailing out of the Grand Harbor. He looted some of their loot so that his *quiraca* would be happy staying home and building herself a fine new home with his profits.

There follows the story of the three Capuchin priests captured by the Moors, who sailed off to North Africa with them as slaves. Contreras caught the ship, saved the Capuchins, sold the Moors to the order, and gave the proceeds to his *quiraca*. He then captured a wealthy Athenian Turk on the high seas, who was ransomed through a dramatic but courteous negotiation, with the threat of a Turkish man-of-war a few hours away and counterfeit money being supplied by a Venetian merchant. All ended happily, with Contreras and the Turks dining together and vying with each other in exchanging gifts and freeing slaves. War was war, but the protagonists were able to rise above the hostility on occasion.

Contreras spoke Greek fluently and often visited the Greek islands, even those within the Turkish sphere of interest: These had at least one visit a year from a Turkish captain of the sea who came to collect taxes and settle any problems that had arisen; for the rest, they were left alone. Contreras made many friends on these islands, and he was treated royally when he dropped anchor. Some insisted on being baptized by him at every visit to justify a celebration and an exchange of gifts. Contreras also undertook occasional cliff-hanging escapes from imminent capture, often using some trick and always relying on the Turks' poor discipline and seamanship. Though he did not always win, he always had the good luck to save his skin, even if bargaining with the Moors was not always easy and sometimes ended in mutual cruelty. On one occasion, the Moors tore the hearts out of the dead to take to Mecca and murdered the living prisoners, while Contreras, in reaction, tied his prisoners back to back and threw them into the sea—all this after peaceful exchanges had been made of sacks of biscuits for barrels of water.

Contreras tells the story of how the grand master called him and told him to go and capture the Jewish tax collector of Salonica and bring him to Malta—"just as though he had asked me to go to the local market and buy some pears," Contreras adds wryly. The reason for this was that whenever the Grand Turk planned an expedition in Christian waters and intended to call together all the Islamic fleets, he put a tax squeeze on his Jewish subjects to pay for it. This, in fact, was almost as easy as going to market, and the news that the Grand Turk planned to bombard Venice was learned. On their way home, they met with a little Greek freighter, whose captain told them that there were no dangers in those waters because Soliman, bey of Chios (and later bey of Algeria) had sailed off, leaving his wife (or, rather, concubine—a beautiful Hungarian girl) at home on Despalmadores Island. Contreras's second in command suggested they capture her, too, which turned out to be just as easy as the first exploit. However, the outcome was that the bey, convinced that Contreras had raped her, put up "Wanted" notices for Contreras in many ports. Some four months later, the Greek second in command was caught and skinned alive, and his skin was then stuffed with straw and attached to the main gate of the city of Rhodes. The Hungarian girl was ransomed by Soliman from the Order of Malta in due course.

Coming back from an expedition, Contreras found his *quiraca* in bed with a friend of his. He ran his sword through him (though not mortally) and he escaped as did the *quiraca*. Contreras refused to take her back, noting with amusement that the other *quiracas* were "fighting over him as though he were some vacant post in the government." After a last, grand raid, which brought him a big bounty, Contreras's thoughts turned to Madrid, to home, and to his mother to whom he had never written. The grand master bid him a fond farewell. Both knew that this was a long-term departure rather than a brief *au revoir*. It was plain that Contreras wanted to change his lifestyle.

Thus ended one phase of Contreras's life and started the next, which was on land rather than on the sea. His first acts were to ask his mother's blessing, pay for a family feast, distribute gifts to all the family, and then leave to recruit an infantry company—a peaceable enough act in itself, but Contreras found roughnecks in Spain who gave him as much trouble as had the Turks. After a violent misunderstanding with the law enforcer of Cordova, he was thrown out of the town—but not before being noted, admired, and desired by a professional lady named Isabella. Contreras was then twenty-one. Having recruited nearly two hundred men, he marched to Estremadura with his woman, who looked as honest as "a colonel's daughter."

They stopped at a village called Hornachos, where an incident five years later upset his whole world. On this occasion, some arms were found in a cellar by one of his soldiers. Contreras reported this to the supply officer, who ordered him to say nothing about it. Lope de Vega based the play he wrote about Contreras on this incident: *King Without a Kingdom*. A series of misfortunes ended in Contreras becoming a hermit. He was accused of heresy, tortured by the attorney general, and finally escaped from house arrest to gather the proof of his innocence. The middle of the story, however, is long, dramatic, and very Spanish—a period of troubles and one major disaster that occurred during a brief return to Malta.

After trouble with his captain, who was always trying to seduce

Isabella, Contreras's company, which had mostly deserted in protest against the captain, was disbanded, and Contreras returned to Palermo, where he was offered the command of a ship for a few looting enterprises that at first were all successful and highly lucrative. Then came the amphibious assault on Hammamet, Tunisia, where they were chastised by God and lost a thousand men on the beach in a matter of less than three hours at the hands of a hundred ill-armed Moors. The soldiers of Malta and Sicily were as if bewitched, allowing themselves to be slaughtered without even defending themselves. Somebody had bugled the retreat, throwing the attack into chaos, but nobody knew who had blown the signal.

Contreras stayed on in Palermo and raised another infantry company. He married a rich lady from Madrid (he was twenty-six) and they lived happily for eighteen months, until Contreras found her and his best friend in bed together. He killed both of them and then left for Spain, where he was nominated sergeant major of Sardinia and, at the same time, had the promotion taken away by an envious functionary at the Escurial, who also had him banned from the palace and from seeing Don Philip III, the king.

By this time, Contreras's spirits were plainly at a low ebb, and he came to terms with his conscience and decided to retire from the world, become a hermit, and thus finish his days. He bought all the necessities and left Madrid with two mules without telling a soul of his intentions or destination. As always, controversy soon arose over his decision among the local Franciscans, but there, at least, no blood was drawn. He went to their convent to hear mass every day, and he begged for oil, bread, and garlic in the village, which, along with some mountain herbs, made up his total diet. He lived this way for seven months and, as he says, "Had I been allowed to stay till today and not been dragged away, I would have been working miracles!"

At this point, the incident involving the Hornachos arms cache in a cellar took place. A magistrate heard about it by chance and started an inquiry. In no time, Contreras was tracked down to his hermitage and a warrant for his arrest issued, accusing him of being king of the Moriscos. A posse captured him, chained him on a donkey, and, under the heavy guard of twelve musketeers, took him to Madrid, where he was interrogated. He immediately offered to be taken by the police to Hornachos to try to find the cellar, which transpired. All was apparently over, except for the statement of the supply officer that he had never been in Hornachos in all his life. Contreras was put on the rack in full Inquisition style to find out who was lying. He won out, though it cost him ten days abed to mend his muscles and his bones.

Then Contreras heard that the supply officer was bribing a whole gang of false witnesses to appeal the case: The supply officer was both very rich and still in jail. So Contreras, dressed as a courier, secretly left Madrid on foot in search of one or more of his soldiers who knew the truth. He succeeded in finding several and had them swear an affidavit in front of a military attorney. He got back to Madrid, where he not only saved his good name but also was promoted by the king to the rank of captain, with his choice of venue. He chose Flanders.

In Flanders, Contreras was choosing a land completely new to him; he went on garrison duty at Cambrai, where nothing happened for two years—not even a little swordplay over a *quiraca* worthy of mention.

Contreras relates, however, an involved story of seeing a ghost—an official horsed courier who arrived during the night, bringing the news that the French king, Henry IV, had been assassinated. This news turned out to be false or rather premature, as the king was, in fact, assassinated nine days later, precisely where and how the ghost courier had stated.

Presumably bored with Flanders, despite a summer campaign, Contreras asked permission to go to Malta. Even this journey was not without its drama. Having little money, he dressed up as a pilgrim and hid a sword inside his staff. At Chalons, he spent too long admiring the city's fortification and was arrested as a spy. His sword was found, and he would certainly have been hanged had he not also hidden a laissez-passer written by the duke of Condé, who was a cousin of the king. He was released and given a military escort to the French frontier at Chambery with all expenses paid. From there, he went to Genoa, then to Naples and Palermo. Finding a tepid welcome in Palermo, he proceeded to Malta, where he carried out a scouting mission by sea and then was honored by being received into the order as a brother servant-at-arms without having to present any documents of service or birth, because he had been so well known for so many years. After a year's novitiate, he received the habit of the order, over the objections of two knights who complained about his homicides. To celebrate his new honors, he returned to Madrid, where he received orders to join the royal fleet. He stayed with it for a few months and then returned to Madrid. There an unhappy incident took place in which Contreras, infuriated by gossip concerning his love affair with a married woman, ended up in jail for slashing the rear end of the lady responsible with his sword. Here, Contreras managed to take advantage of the law that members of the Order of Malta could opt for trial by members of their own priory. Such a trial took place, and Contreras was banished from Madrid for two years and went to serve in the fleet. Still looking for promotion, he returned to Madrid, where his name was, not surprisingly, overlooked. He decided to return to Malta, but even this journey held its surprises.

In Rome, Contreras fell sick of malaria, but because he was not sick abed, he went to visit some Spanish ladies he knew. Some Italian knights burst into the house and threatened Contreras, who responded with his sword, starting a battle sufficiently noisy to attract the police, who arrested them all. In front of the governor, however, all shook hands, promising to forget the affair. Then the Italian knights decided to poison Contreras with arsenic prescribed by a phony doctor. By good luck and the quick wits of his traveling companion, Contreras was saved by the Portuguese doctor who worked for the Spanish embassy. All these incidents, perhaps not world-shaking in their importance, are fleshed out by Contreras with the human detail that brings them alive after four centuries. One is tempted to sympathize with Contreras's reasoning and reactions, but one tends to have a certain reserve with regard to the heavy hand he used to resolve his problems. In any case, Contreras arrived back in Madrid to find that a cousin of his was raising an infantry company in his name and in his stead, on the understanding that if Alonso de Contreras did not arrive in time he would command it. This cousin was chagrined at Contreras's arrival and decided to kill him: He corrupted Contreras's page boy, who was to put arsenic and sugar in his food. The tale is long and complex: The boy was found out, caught, and given only a whipping, while the cousin vanished to the Philippines, leaving no forwarding address. They got away lightly with their crime, as Contreras, on his believed deathbed, told his confessor that he forgave his murderers. For two years after the poisoning, he suffered from pain in his hands and feet.

After this misfortune, Contreras suffered yet another. Given the military command of a galleon, he, with other ships, left Cádiz to block a Dutch fleet that was expected to raid the coast. It never arrived, and Contreras ran his own ship onto a reef by Cádiz Harbor. Then, with orders and counterorders, he sailed not for the Philippines but for the Caribbean. The Spanish high command would seem to have been fickle, with its continuous alterations of plans and, oddly to us nowadays, its continuous transfer of officers from duty with the fleet to duty in the land forces. The troops he had aboard were on the point of mutiny, when Contreras, with a mixture of violence and cunning, terrified them into obedience. On this mission, Contreras was nearing thirty-five years of age; his orders were to visit Puerto Rico, Santo Domingo, and Cuba, leaving some soldiers and military stores at each garrison. The soldiers considered their postings as life imprisonment or the death penalty. On arrival at Puerto Rico, Contreras learned that Sir Walter Raleigh and five ships were pirating up and down the islands, so he laid a trap for them. Dressing up his ships as merchantmen and co-opting a couple of freighters he furnished with cannons, Contreras sailed out of port with ships that looked like easy prey. Soon the English crowded in on his little fleet, at which point he hoisted the Spanish flag and opened fire. The battle was far from conclusive: Contreras lost nothing, and the English lost a sea captain. The English ships were faster and better handled than those of the Spaniards. In all events, Contreras found a small ship, manned by twenty-one English sailors, hiding in a creek. He captured the sailors and sent them back to Spain as prisoners. They told him that Raleigh was a broken man, after the loss of his son during an expedition to Brazil, and that he was going home. In fact, he was shortly thereafter hanged in London for piracy on the high seas, after complaints from the Spanish government.

Back in Cádiz, Contreras found himself under orders to prepare six heavy galleons and two fleet tenders for a long voyage carrying a thousand men. These set sail and a few days later were hit by a storm that blew them back onto the Spanish coast, destroying all the galleons and throwing their cannons onto the beach. Contreras manned two schooners and went fishing for the cannons. This was important, as the Algerians were standing by, waiting for the moment when they could do the same. This competition for the cannons was based on their technological superiority. The Turks and the Moors could not cast cannons of the quality that the Spaniards could; this gave the Spaniards firepower superiority in every engagement.

The two schooners soon came in useful. The Spaniards held a river port (chiefly for buying mutton, beef, chicken, and corn cheaply) called Mámora on the Atlantic coast of Morocco. It was under siege by thirty thousand Moors and twenty-eight galleys, half Turkish and half Dutch. The garrison had no ammunition left and was awaiting the coup de grace.

Contreras planned to arrive at dawn and jump his schooners

over the sandbars with the surf, before the besieging fleet was aware of his arrival. "I was like the dove, bringing the good news back to the Ark," he remarked of his felicitous arrival. The enemy galleys started melting away, convinced that the Spanish fleet would arrive before long, which it did, the morning after. The Moorish chieftains came to heel, promising to leave during the night, but not before all of Contreras's men and all of the gunpowder kegs had been filed past the window of the room where the peace treaty agreement was to be made, which would include the Spaniards buying five hundred sheep and thirty cows at rock-bottom prices.

This exploit was a scoop for Contreras, who took the news personally on horseback to the king in Madrid, traveling two hundred miles in three and a half days. He was received by the king and was offered a promotion and a standing ovation by the Council of State. However, as happened in all high places, the king, pope, or prince received petitioners in open audience, and he would promote, honor, and make promises in public that were words only. The petitioner's problem was to make sure that the ministers, monsignori, or archivists wrote the promise down clearly. Here the problem became difficult; the king, for example, might be too generous with money he had not got, or give promotions and jobs that did not exist or were already filled. All such promises had to be cut down to size by the administrators: The king had made the generous gesture, and that was all that mattered. In any event, Contreras had the misfortune of the minister concerned dropping dead from a thrombosis in his office and of everybody saying it was Contreras's fault, "just as though I had let him have a volley with my culverin."

After a while, Contreras was posted to a galleon, the *Admiral of Naples,* along with two hundred soldiers, to block a Dutch fleet aiming to enter the Mediterranean at Gibraltar. The battle started and Admiral Ribera's galleon was holed on the water line. It was not hit by an enemy ship, and the enemy laughed with scorn at the Spaniards. Then came a time when there really were no vacant posts, troops to be recruited, or ships to be manned. At this time, Contreras met the famous Spanish playwright Lope de Vega, who housed him for eight months and who wrote *King Without a Kingdom* about Contreras's hermitage period, as previously mentioned. Considering that living in Madrid, at the court, was no place for a soldier, especially one without money, Contreras sought permission to return to Malta, but even this journey brought yet another new facet to his life. He became governor of Pantelleria, a small (now Italian) island that lies between Sicily and Tunis. This position was conferred on him by the viceroy of Sicily.

This unusual appointment, because of its geographical position close to the Barbary Coast, entailed considerable danger: Even in very recent times, Libya fired two rockets at the island from the African mainland, fortunately causing no injury, but this demonstrates how little has changed over the centuries. In all events, the viceroy must have thought that Contreras's reputation as a warrior would, of itself, protect the indefensible little isle, but Contreras was thinking quite differently—he was thinking of retiring from battle and retiring once and for all.

While Contreras was governor of this isle, which still today produces some of the best strong muscat wine in the world, he completely restored the little church and sacristy there, bringing materials and craftsmen from Sicily and endowing the church with money to pay for masses, high, low, and sung, in perpetuity, for his soul and those of others in purgatory. Having seen to it that the church was the most handsome building on the island, he asked permission to go to Rome to see if there was any way to get round the regulations of the Order of Malta and become a pensioner with a commandery.

Rome and the count of Monterey (Spanish ambassador extraordinary to the papacy) changed Contreras's life unexpectedly. First, he was received in audience by Pope Urban VIII, who was so moved by the remarkable life of this warrior that he loaded him with honors as well as a brief instructing the Order of Malta to receive him as a knight of justice with all the privileges of seniority and commanderies and a perpetually indulgenced altar in his church on Pantelleria. The only problem was that the Vatican's administrative monsignori thought the pope had been overgenerous and tried to hedge his honors, but the count of Monterey took up Contreras's case and not only obtained everything that the pope had promised but put him on his staff at a good salary. He allowed Contreras to make a quick trip to Malta to get his papers in order as a knight, after which he became a sort of bodyguard front man who inspired respect and more than a little awe. Monterey, though very rich and grandiose in his actions, was short and unimpressive personally: He therefore needed a tough image up front.

Contreras organized the travel and visit of three cardinals from Spain and that of the marquis of Cadreyta, Spanish ambassador to the queen of Hungary: All was done with much grandeur. He was sent to Madrid as a bodyguard to Monterey's secretary, on an important mission during which he finally saw some of Lope de Vega's plays and understood the great honor the playwright had done him.

The count of Monterey then became viceroy of Naples, and Contreras, with a company of Spanish veterans, became the viceroy's bodyguard. Some months later, they were sent to garrison the little town of Nola that lies behind the volcano Vesuvius. For anyone else, this would have been a dull visit to a duller provincial town, but for Contreras it was dramatic and dangerous. Vesuvius erupted. It rained balls of fire and ashes; the earth shook, crumbling the houses while the noise of the trees being uprooted added to the terror. The sun was hidden by smoke, and all the road communications were cut. This Nola earthquake is well recorded in history books for its violence and destruction. Even some of Contreras's well-disciplined troops mutinied out of fear. It was like Judgment Day, with streams of lava pouring down the mountainside, one of which Contreras and some soldiers managed to deviate before it reached the town of Nola. Finally, orders came from the count for them to retreat to Capua, where they arrived "looking like men who had been working in hell."

Contreras had been made a knight of justice, and he liked to administer justice in his own way: He tells an entertaining story of how he quartered his troops. He found that he could only put them in the houses of the poor and never of the rich, because the rich always had a family member who was a cleric and who had taken deacon's orders and whose home was thus exempt from having Spanish troops billeted in them. This was a trick, because these deacons played no religious role and were usually married and had children. Ignoring this privilege, Contreras billeted his unwelcome Spanish veterans, giving orders that the cleric's room should be respected "like the Day of the Lord." All the rich complained to the archbishop, but, for all that, it took over a month for the orders to arrive from Naples to withdraw the troops and for the archbishop to withdraw his threat to excommunicate Contreras, who wrote to the archbishop, "If I get myself excommunicated, nobody will be safe from me: For that very purpose, God gave me ten fingers and five hundred Spanish veterans."

His second little sally into social justice was when he was appointed governor of Aquila, a rebellious city in the mountains where bandits ruled the countryside. Contreras had the bandits whipped, washed in saltwater (an old Spanish navy punishment) and sent to be galley slaves. The chief brigand was then captured and executed, to the astonishment of all, in the city's main piazza. In another strike for social justice, Contreras stopped the habit of the city's rich aldermen of increasing the price of food and taxes and demanding that the shopkeepers supply them free. He allowed the price increases and then forced all the rich to buy for cash in proportion to their wealth and household. But his egalitarian views were not appreciated, and Contreras was given back his command of the viceroy's bodyguard squadron of cavalry.

Even this did not go smoothly. He had a quarrel and an im-
promptu duel with Don Hector Piñatelo, who had been commander of the squadron, when Contreras accused him of
switching the horses and leaving him a lot of old mares; the duel
ended in a three-day house arrest for both parties and an injunc-
tion to make peace.

Contreras's next public appearance was at the head of a grand
military parade in the heart of Naples; he and his troopers were
in grandiose new uniforms with the colors of Monterey, followed
by 2,500 cavalrymen, 2,700 Spanish infantrymen and 8,000 Italian regular troops, after which there was a mock battle with
realistic artillery fire. For sheer spectacle and grandiosity, Contreras concludes that there was no prince to rival the count of
Monterey. Next morning, however, Contreras was sent with five
hundred cavalrymen to defend the area south of Naples from a
threatened Turkish landing, which, in fact, never materialized.
During this mission, he has only the miraculous tales of two
horses to tell, one a cavalry charger so violent that nobody could
approach it, which he gave to some Franciscan friars who harnessed it with a mare and the two ploughed together happily ever
after. The other was about a good-tempered mare that one day
just refused, like a mule, to move. A trooper had barely taken
Contreras's place on the saddle when the mare charged straight at
a stone wall, killing both horse and rider. Contreras gave thanks
to God for his good fortune.

At this time, Contreras aimed to wind up his affairs and his
career, his only major concern being to get a promotion, pay, and
a posting for a younger brother—a task that caused him to
quarrel with various authorities. He himself was ready to take up
residence in his commandery in the province of Leon. First,
Monterey offered him the governorship of Pescara, a most important post and a great temptation to postpone his departure, but,
then, after making him wait a long time, he asked Contreras to
refit two little galleons and a fleet tender and do some piracy
among the Greek islands. Contreras agreed, with the proviso that

his brother command at least the fleet tender, to which the viceroy agreed. Later, the viceroy reneged on this, and Contreras retired to a local monastery, where he continued a correspondence with the viceroy, who finally gave him permission to leave for Malta, but asking him the courtesy of telling him where his warships should go with the greatest likelihood of good loot.

Contreras records that "he passed a penitential two months in the monastery, with four masses in the morning and vespers in the evening, and, for lunch and dinner, a chicken and excellent old wine and everything that went with it." He added that rumors reached Malta that he had become a Capuchin friar and that he had even been seen celebrating mass.

Contreras took leave of the viceroy and coasted down Calabria. At Paola Port, he not only visited the big convent of St. Francis of Paola but also met a young Spanish lady who was traveling in the other direction. Saying she was frightened to be alone, she asked Contreras to dine with her and to sleep in her cabin. The next morning's dialogue was: "What a wicked old man you are, by Jesus."

"Yes, no doubt," Contreras replied, "and I am sure you would have preferred a younger man to look at in the morning."

Finally, Contreras reached Palermo. His brother was sent off to Flanders, and on 4 February 1633 Contreras wrote that he was fifty-one years old. Soon, all the documents arrived from Malta conferring on him the estates and commandery of San Juan de Puente de Orbi, and he boarded a galley to Barcelona via Naples. At Naples, as soon as he showed the documents regarding his commandery, all was forgiven and the viceroy urged him to stay, but having his baggage at the bottom of the ship's hold was a polite excuse for refusing.

Back in Spain, the first thing Contreras did was to take possession of his commandery and try again to resolve the problems of his younger brother's career, which had been blocked by Pedro de Arce, an old enemy who accused Contreras of having falsified his papers, a charge that Contreras had to disprove before his brother was promoted.

"In February 1633, when I am writing this," he went on, "if God grants me longer life and if anything of interest happens, I shall add it to this story."

Perhaps he lived happily ever after in his commandery, but I doubt it.

CHAPTER ONE

I was born in that most noble city of Madrid on 6 January 1582.

I was baptized in the parish of San Miguel de la Sagra. My godparents were Alonso de Roa and Maria de Roa; they were my mother's brother and sister. My parents were called Grabiel Guillén and Juana de Roa y Contreras.

I went to serve the king when I was still only a child, and, knowing no better, I took my mother's name instead of my father's. When I discovered the mistake I had made, I could not correct it, as the name *Contreras* was already written on my papers of service. Contreras, then, I have been since that day, and it is under that name I am known, despite the fact that I was named Alonso Guillén at my baptism.

My parents were poor and they were *Old Christians,* with no taint of Moorish or Jewish blood; they had never been accused of heresy by the Holy Office of the Inquisition. (Later on I will show you the importance of this to me.) My mother and father lived together for twenty-four years, married according to the laws of our Holy Mother Church. They had sixteen children and when my father died eight of us, six sons and two daughters, were left. I was the eldest of them all, though still a schoolboy.

† I KILL A BOY †

There were, in Madrid, at the time of my father's death, some jousting tournaments by the Segovia Bridge. All the town came to gape like idiots at them as though jousting had never been seen before. Another boy named Salvador Moreno, the son of a court police officer, and I missed school one day to see the jousting.

The next day, when I returned to school, the master told me, "You're a good boy, Alonso; just come up here and pull down Moreno's breeches so I can beat him."

Unsuspectingly, I went up. Then, the teacher treacherously came up behind me. "Alonso," he said, "take down your breeches!"

But without waiting for me to do so, he gave me a whipping that drew blood.

It turned out that this punishment had been asked for by the father of my school friend and that the teacher whipped only me for the truancy. He had no better reason than that Salvador's father was richer than mine had been.

On leaving school that day, we went to the Concibción Jerónima square, our usual playground. As the whipping was still burning, I drew my penknife, threw Salvador facedown on the ground, and jabbed him in the back. As it seemed that I had done him no harm, I turned him over and dug him in the tripes. All the other boys said that I had killed him, so I took to my heels and that night returned home as if nothing had happened.

That evening, my mother had given each of us a penny bun, and while we were eating someone knocked sharply at the door.

"Who is there?" my mother asked.

"The law," was the answer.

Immediately, I ran upstairs to the top of the house and squeezed myself under my mother's bed. The police officer Moreno came into the house, searched everywhere, found me, and dragged me from under the bed with a twist of his wrist.

"You little devil," he said, "you knifed my son!"

I was next led off to the Court prison, where I was questioned. I denied everything.

The next day, I had to appear in court with twenty-two other children who had also been arrested. The clerk of the court read out a charge which accused me of having stabbed the boy with my penknife. I denied it, and said that some other boy must have done it. Every boy swore that he had not done it, and soon fistfights broke out. It was no small job for the officials to put an end to the riot and clear the courtroom.

However, the end of the business was that the boy's father talked at such length and so persuasively in court that within two days he proved me guilty. My being only fourteen years old was a great subject for discussion among the judges. My being so young, in fact, and only that, saved me. I was condemned to a year's exile from the court and not allowed to come within fifteen miles of Madrid at the risk of having my period of exile doubled.

The court police officer lost his son, who died on the day that I was sentenced, and I was immediately sent off to take my punishment. I spent my year of exile at Avila with my uncle, who was the rector of the church of Santiago in that city. When I had completed my year, I returned to Madrid.

† FROM SCULLION TO DESERTER †

Within twenty days of my return home, the Prince Cardinal Albert arrived in Madrid. He had been governor of Portugal and was on his way to Flanders, where he had just been appointed governor.

"Señora, I want to go to the wars with the cardinal," I said to my mother.

"Don't be a silly boy," she replied, "you're scarcely out of your cradle and now you want to go off fighting. No, you're going to be a silversmith: I had you apprenticed to one only today."

I told her that I did not want to serve any master but the king. But despite that she took me along to the silversmith who had made this agreement with my mother unbeknownst to me.

My mother left me at his house. The first thing that happened was that the silversmith's wife gave me a copper jar, and no small one at that, and told me to go and draw water at the los Caños del Peral fountain.

"I am here," I said to her, "as an apprentice; not as a servant. Send whom you like to get water, but not *me*."

She took off one of her wooden clogs and raised it to hit me. I countered by picking up the copper jar and throwing it at her. However I did her no harm as I was not then strong enough.

I quickly ran down the shop's steps and headed for home. When I arrived I shouted at my mother, "Must I disgrace myself and carry buckets of water through the town?"

Then the silversmith arrived, all prepared to give me a whipping. I ran away and quickly collected lots of stones and started to pelt him with them.

Some people came upon me unexpectedly, and I was caught. When the trouble was all explained, they said that they could not understand why I should be forced to do what I obviously did not want to do. The silversmith was persuaded by them, and I stayed with my mother. I then said to her, "Señora, you are burdened with so many of us children. Why not let me go and earn my living under the prince?"

Resigning herself, my mother said, "But I have nothing to give you, my boy."

Even if my mother had divided all her possessions, her dowry excepted, there would only have been six hundred *reales* to share between the eight of us. That was a very small sum.

"That doesn't matter," I replied. "With God's help, I'll earn enough for us all."

Nevertheless, she bought me a shirt and some leather shoes and gave me four *reales* and her blessing.

With all these things, on Tuesday, the seventh of September 1595, at dawn, I left Madrid as a camp follower behind the trumpets of the prince cardinal.

Contreras seems a little doubtful of the history of his first campaign. Fourteen years before his departure, the Protestant provinces of the Spanish Netherlands—Holland and Zeeland being the most important—had revolted and only Flanders remained loyal to Spain. Since then, there had been continuous fighting. Only three years before Contreras left, Queen Elizabeth of England had sent a force to this area under the Earl of Leicester and had defeated the Spaniards. Currently, Henry IV of France was attacking the provinces from the south and had already captured Amiens and Picardy.

As Alonso walked out of Madrid, he was not yet a soldier. He was taking a gamble with his life and, boylike, hoped that something would happen quickly. It was a common view that only destitutes became soldiers, and it was perhaps this that motivated his actions that evening.

That night we stopped at Alcalá de Henares. I went to a church where there was a great festa in honor of the prince cardinal. And it was there, in the crowd, that I found a toffee seller with some playing cards. Like a hardened gambler, I unlaced my shirt, brought out my four *reales* from the pocket inside, and challenged him to a game.

Soon I lost my four *reales,* and after that I lost my new shirt. Then, with a run of ill luck, I lost the new shoes that I had kept safely tucked in my belt. I asked the merchant if he wanted to play me for my old hood, and in a moment he had that, too. There I was, destitute, which is what I suppose I wanted to be. Then a man standing nearby who had been watching the game asked the merchant to give me a *real*. The merchant good-humoredly did so, and gave me a stick of toffee for luck. I was so delighted that I felt as though I were the winner after all.

That evening, I went to the palace—well, if not to the palace, at least to the palace kitchens to get warm by the fires. It was a cold night. I had slipped in with the kitchen boys.

In the morning, the trumpets blew for the twelve-mile march to Guadalajara. I bought some sweet fritters with what remained of my last *real* and lived on them until we reached Guadalajara. On the march, I asked the kitchen boys to have pity on me and let me ride on the kitchen wagon for a while. But they would have nothing to do with me just because I was not one of their profession.

We arrived at Guadalajara. I went to the palace again because I had found the kitchen fires very pleasant the night before. I then insinuated myself, without being asked, into helping pluck the birds and turning the spits. By that means, as I shall explain, I even had supper that night. Master James, the prince cardinal's cook, finding that I was an obliging and useful boy, asked me where I came from. I told him, and then informed him that I was off to the wars. He immediately ordered his staff to give me a good supper and to let me ride on the kitchen wagon for the next day's march. They allowed me to get on the wagon the next day—but not very willingly.

On the journey, I continued to make myself useful in the kitchen. In fact, I worked so well that Master James took me into his service. I became the favorite of his kitchen and was put in charge of the two large wagons that went at the front of the column with the prince. This gave me the opportunity to take revenge on the kitchen boys who had had no pity on me. I made *them* march. But soon my anger subsided, and I let them aboard.

We took the road as far as Saragossa, where there was a great festa. From there, we went to Montserrat and then on to Barcelona. We stayed in Barcelona for a few days before boarding twenty-six galleys that were sailing for Genoa.

At Villefranche, the duke of Savoy gave us a grand welcome. From there, we sailed to Savona. On this last leg of the journey, we captured a ship. It was probably French—I believe we were at war with France at that time—though she may have been a Moor or a Turk. The artillery battle, which went on before we actually took her, delighted me.

We stayed at Savona for a few days. Then we went to Milan. From there, we took the road through Burgundy to Flanders. On the march, we passed numerous companies of Spanish infantry and cavalry, which made a wonderful sight.

When I saw that some of the soldiers were (or so it seemed to me) as young as I was, I decided to ask Master James to give me permission to leave so I could join the army. But he had taken such a liking to me that he would not let me go. His reply, in fact, was that he was going to give me a good hiding. I was furious.

I immediately presented myself to his highness, the prince cardinal, with a petition detailing everything that had happened to me and what I wanted. Basically, I had followed him from Madrid, his cook would not give me leave, and I did not wish to serve anyone but the king.

He told me that I was still a child. I replied that there were many other "children" in his infantry companies. The next day my petition came back to me, and written on the bottom was, "Let him be enrolled even though he is not of military age."

My master gave up hope only when he saw he could do nothing more to stop me, but he was kind enough to say, "I shall not fail you, and until we get to Flanders come to me for anything you want."

And I did. Thanks to him, I was able to feed more than ten soldiers and most importantly the man in charge of the troop I was in.

I had been enrolled in Captain Mejía's company, and as we were drawing our stores at a time when we were getting near Flanders, my troop leader, a man whom I looked up to in the same way as I looked to the king, said to me one evening, "Follow me; captain's orders."

He put a pack on my back and we set off. Morning came, and

we were fifteen miles away. I asked him where we were going, and he told me we were going to Naples. It turned out that we had deserted the army and that this man was no lover of battles.

I stayed with him in Naples several days, until one morning I found myself bundled aboard a ship bound for Palermo.

CHAPTER TWO

In a very short time, I reached Palermo. Instantly, I was engaged as page and shield carrier to Captain Felipe de Menargas, a Catalan. He looked after me well, and my time with him was very happy.

One day, there was an opportunity to go on an expedition to Greece. Spanish galleys from the kingdom of Naples and from Sicily were sailing. The Neapolitan galleys were under the command of General don Pedro de Toledo, and the galleys of Sicily sailed under don Pedro de Leyva. The companies were ordered to capture a place in Morea called Patras. My captain's company was embarked in the *capitana* of the Sicilian squadron, commanded by Captain Cesare Latorre.

Battles and skirmishes with the Turks and the Moors were everyday affairs but were seldom on any decisively large scale, although the Turks had captured all of Greece and almost all of the Greek islands. Their Moorish subjects also held the coastline from Antioch to Casablanca.

For this expedition, Contreras mentions that he sailed in the capitana *of the Sicilian squadron. The system of command was that each Spanish*

9

naval force had two flagships. The one carrying the senior military officer was called the capitana, *the other carrying the senior naval officer was called the* almiranta.

If, for example, as in this case, a naval force or fleet were made up of two squadrons of galleys, there would be a capitana *and an* almiranta *for the whole fleet. Each of the squadrons would then have one ship designated as the* capitana *and another as the* almiranta, *which would respectively carry the senior military officer and the senior naval officer of the squadron.*

The military side of naval warfare was much stressed in the sixteenth and seventeenth centuries; full-scale military landing operations were commonplace. Galley battles in the Mediterranean were won by hand-to-hand fighting at sea by soldiers rather than by superior seamanship and artillery firepower. When carried to the Atlantic, this military attitude to naval warfare proved disastrous, especially in the case of the Spanish Armada in 1588. Additionally, the Turks never learned the tricks of seamanship that the English perfected.

We arrived at Patras, a town on the west coast of Greece. First, we landed troops to capture and hold the beach, then the light troops threw their scaling ladders against the castle walls to begin the assault. It was here that I first felt cannonballs whistling past my ears as I stood in front of my captain carrying a shield and his gilded lance. (The gilded lance was the sign of the commander's presence.)

We took the countryside easily enough, but not the castle. We also captured plenty of slaves and loot, out of which, greenhorn though I was, I did quite well. If I did not do so well ashore, at least I did well when we got back aboard ship. The soldiers gave me lots of valuables to look after and tipped me generously. (It was a custom of soldiers to make the drummer boy or page look after money, as he never ran away with it.) We had scarcely dropped anchor in Sicily before I had bought myself a suit of many colors.

In Palermo, I met a soldier who told me he was a fellow citizen of mine, and I believed him. He asked to borrow my captain's clothes so he could put on a play. Again I believed him, particularly when he told me that I, too, would be invited to join the party. He quickly carried away lots of clothes, and they were the very fine ones that my master had in his strongbox. Taking his choice of the clothes, he also helped himself to a set of gold buttons and a silken hatband covered with precious stones as well!

When the next morning came, our sergeant told the captain that four men had deserted. One of them, of course, was the soldier who had said he came from Madrid. On hearing this news, my stomach sank.

However, without so much as bat of an eyelash, I went off and made some inquiries and heard that some galleys of the Order of St. John of Jerusalem were in port. I found one and went aboard.

† WE LOOT ON LAND AND SEA †

When we got to Messina, I wrote a letter to my master, the captain, to explain what had happened. I told him that I had not asked his permission to go away because I was afraid. We then sailed on to Malta.

Some Spanish knights were on the same galley, and they kindly arranged to have the grand master of the Order of St. John of Jerusalem's collector of rents and a renowned knight called Gaspar of Monreal, employ me. He was very pleased to take me into his service, and I stayed with him for a year to his entire satisfaction. At the end of this time, I asked him for permission to return to Sicily, as I wanted to become a soldier and because my captain had been writing continuously asking me to rejoin him, saying how much he wished me to return.

Commander Monreal unwillingly gave me leave to go, and he sent me off looking very smart in a brand new suit of clothes. I arrived at Messina, where the viceroy, the duke of Maqueda, was staying at the time, and I enrolled as a soldier in my master's company. And this time I served him as a soldier and no longer as a page boy or personal servant.

A year later, the viceroy had a galliot* fitted for action. He gave instructions for four days' pay to be given to every soldier who volunteered to man it. I was one of them. We sailed to the Barbary Coast. The ship's captain was Ruy Pérez de Mercado. We found nothing on the coast, but on our way back we came on a ship almost as big as ours at anchor at an island called Lampadusa.

We rowed into the anchorage, captured the ship with scarcely a shot fired, and not only did we take the ship but also the greatest of all the corsairs as well, a man named Caradali, and, with him, we caught ninety Turks.

We got a fine welcome at Palermo from the viceroy, and our success whetted his appetite for further ventures. Subsequently, he commissioned two large galleons: One he named the *Golden Galleon* and the other the *Silver Galleon*.

I embarked on the *Golden Galleon* and went to the Levant in her. We captured so many ships that it would take too long to describe it all, and we returned rich, every one of us. As a soldier on three *escudos* a month, I brought back three hundred, part in silver, part in kind. And that was not counting the hat full to the brim with pieces of two that I got for my share of the booty, which the viceroy ordered to be distributed among us all when we were back in Palermo.

This gave me all the self confidence in the world. But in a very few days, it was all gambled away or wasted in extravagances.

Again the two galleons were sent to the Levant. There, we made some incredible lootings on land and sea. The viceroy's

---

* *A small galley; a fighting ship used in the Mediterranean, employing both oars and sail as means of propulsion.*

luck still held. We sacked the warehouses of Alexandretta, the seaport to which all the merchandise came from Portuguese India by way of Babylon and Aleppo. We again brought back immense wealth.

During these travels, I hardly slept. I fell in love with the art of navigation. I spent all my time asking the navigators questions. I also used to watch them tracing their charts. I made myself familiar with the countries, the capes, and the ports, noting each as we sailed past. This groundwork served me well many years later when I made a full series of survey charts of the Levant, Morea, Anatolia, Caramania, Syria, and Africa as far as Cape Cantin in the Atlantic. I also drew up charts of the islands of Crete, Cyprus, Sardinia, Majorca, and Minorca. These *portolan* charts also included the coast of Spain from Cape St. Vincent and followed the coastline past Sanlucar and Gibraltar to Carthagena, Barcelona, and then the coast of France as far as Marseilles. From there the charts covered Genoa and on to Leghorn and the Tiber and Naples. All the coast of Calabria as far as Apulia and up to the Gulf of Venice, port by port, was done with the capes and natural harbors marked. They all showed where various types of ships could shelter and in how great a depth of water. Prince Filibert now has all fourteen of them.

† I FLEE TO NAPLES FOR SAFETY †

We reached Palermo safely with all our loot. The viceroy was delighted. He gave us our share, and we were well sewn up with gold. We were known as the viceroy's Levantines, and, with this swashbuckling title, no one dared to deny us anything. To enjoy our prestige to the full, we used to go from tavern to tavern and bawdy house to bawdy house.

One evening, however, we were carousing in a tavern, as

was our custom, and one of my companions (for there were three of us) said to the innkeeper, "Bring us something to eat, you sod."

The innkeeper said that he was nothing of the sort and refused to move a step. One of my friends drew his knife and stabbed him, and the innkeeper never rose again.

Everyone in the room attacked us with roasting spits and any weapon they could lay their hands on. It was fortunate for us that we knew how to defend ourselves, and we finally saved our skins by hiding in the church of Nuestra Señora de Gruta. There we stayed waiting to hear how the viceroy would take it. We then heard that he had said, "I shall hang them when I catch them."

"My friends," I said to my companions, "it is safer to hide in the woods than to trust in the prayers of good men." (This was an old Spanish proverb.)

So we pooled our money, which made a miserable sum. Then I sent them for our muskets without even having a plan.

The church was on the coast—in fact, it was right on the port—so when we had our muskets I made use of my knowledge of the sea and assessed all the ships in the harbor and chose a sailing bark that was loaded with sugar. At midnight, I said to my companions, "Now is the time to go aboard, if you feel so disposed, gentlemen."

"But we'll be heard," said one of the company.

"There's only a cabin boy aboard," I told them.

We went down and got aboard. One of us put his hand over the cabin boy's mouth and, weighing anchor, said to him, "Keep quiet or we'll kill you."

We got out the oars and began to leave the jetty. As we got within hailing distance of the castle, a sentry challenged us, and we replied in Italian, "Fishing boat!"

This seemed to satisfy him, as we heard no more from him. We set our sails for Naples, a distance of three hundred miles, and by the grace of God we got there in three days.

† TROUBLE IN NAPLES, TOO †

The harbormaster came to see our papers, and we told him the truth. We told him that we had fled because we were afraid of being hanged by the duke of Maqueda.

The viceroy of Naples was the count of Lemos, and his son was the captain of infantry. He was called Don Francisco de Castro. This son later became viceroy of Sicily and is the present count of Lemos, although he has now become a monk.

The count sent for us. Having looked us over, he remarked that we were a good-looking trio, and he conscripted us on the spot for his son's foot company, giving orders that the bark and the sugar should be sent back to Palermo.

The Neapolitans also called us the Levantines of the duke of Maqueda and gave us the reputation of being men who did not know the meaning of mercy.

We had a few days, however, with a respectable reputation in Naples. That was because we three lived alone and encouraged no visitors! However, one evening a Valencian from the same company as ours and a friend of his called on us. They were, if we were to believe them, real *caballeros*.

"Come with us, please," they said, "as we have had some serious trouble in the Florentines' quarters."

So, not wishing to lose our reputation of the Levantines, we shouted, "By the Christ, lead us to them!"

On the road, we passed a man loitering. I assumed him to be awaiting some amorous assignation. The Valencians were lagging behind us and, when we heard a shout and turned back to see what was happening, we saw one of the Valencians coming toward us carrying a cape and a sombrero.

"There's a swine that will grunt no more," he said.

"What was it all about?" I asked him.

"Nothing," he replied, "he was just a pig I sent to dine with the devil and who has kindly bequeathed me this cape."

When I heard what he said, I was scandalized and, going up to one of my friends, I said, "For God's sake, have we come out on a looting expedition? It is certainly not what I came for."

"Patience, please, just for once," my friend replied. "We must not lose our reputation in front of these spirited gentlemen."

"To the devil with this reputation!" I said.

We got to a house where they sold wine. It was there, as we soon learned, that the Valencians had had their troubles. We went in by a side door, our Valencians barging in, talking loudly in order to create a disturbance. Then they buffeted the innkeeper, made sword thrusts at the carafes and wineskins, of which there were dozens about, pinking some, smashing others, so that the wine flowed like a red river.

The innkeeper shouted through the window for help, while by a small door we got out to the road. Then someone threw a flowerpot from the inn; it hit one of my companions, knocking him senseless. In answer to the shouts for help, an Italian patrol arrived, and we started a hand-to-hand battle with them. My companion who had been hit by the flowerpot still could not get up: He had been laid well and truly. In the end, the Italians pressed us back with their muskets and halberds. They smashed the fist of one of the Valencians with a halberd blow and captured him, and with him my companion who was still laid out on the ground. The rest of us then broke into retreat toward our lodgings.

As the Italian patrol was leading the prisoners away, they came across the corpse from which the Valencian had taken the cape and hat. Immediately, word was sent to the Spanish main guard, and a search party was sent out for my companion, myself, and the other Valencian.

After we had said farewell to the Valencian, we went back to our house to collect our few possessions before decamping. But there in front of our door we saw a military patrol with lighted lanterns waiting for us.

"It's every man for himself now, my friend," I said. "If you had listened to me when the Valencian stole the cape and sombrero, we would not now be on the run."

With that, I rushed down an alleyway and made for the jetty. In a short time, I got to the inn, which was right in front of the customhouse, where I knew there was a knight of St. John staying who had come from Malta to arm a galleon to go to the Levant.

This knight turned out to be my old friend Captain Betrian.

He was delighted to see me. When I told him truthfully what had happened, he hid me. I remained hidden for the twenty days until he sailed. On the twentieth night, he took me aboard and hid me in the biscuit store, where I sweated blood and water until we got clear of Naples. He then brought me up from the hold, and we arrived safely in Malta.

The Valencian and my friend who was felled by the flowerpot were both hanged within ten days. As for the others, I have never heard of them again.

CHAPTER THREE

Commander Monreal was very pleased to see me again when I got to Malta, but we were there only a few days before we set off for the Levant with the same galleon and a frigate. We were two months at sea without a smell of the enemy. But one day in a creek near Cape Silidonia, when we were just going to drop anchor, we came upon a handsome-looking caramousel,* which had rather the lines of a galleon.

Straightaway, we attacked her. The Turkish crew jumped into their boats and made for the shore. Immediately our captain offered us ten *escudos* a head for every live Turk we could bring back. I was among the soldiers to accept his offer, and we leapt ashore after the Turks.

I concealed myself and waited in a pinewood. Then, a gargantuan Turk passed by and I jumped on him. A real savage he was. He was trying to rally his men at the time by waving an orange and white flag in the air, which he had fixed onto his pike.

A Turkish ship used for cargo carrying, but often carrying artillery and soldiers for defensive purposes.

I poked him with my sword and said in Arabic to him, "Lie down on the ground."

This gargantuan Turk looked at me and started to laugh. At that time, though I was equipped with a sword and a shield, I had a face as smooth as a girl's.

"Go away, you little whore," he said, "your bottom stinks like a dead dog."

My anger mounted, and, picking up my shield, I went for him. With one thrust, I knocked the pike out of his hand and struck him in the chest with my sword. He fell to the ground, and I tore the flag off his pike and wound it round my middle.

While I was beginning to rob the Turk, up came two French soldiers shouting, "Divide three ways."

I stood up and, protecting myself with my shield, said threateningly, "You leave him alone. He's all mine. And if you try to do anything I will run you through."

Well, we were beginning a nice fight when four soldiers, with three Turks they had captured, came upon us and made peace. We all went back to the galleon together, carrying my Turk but without stripping him of his possessions.

The whole story was told to the captain, and he confirmed it by talking to the Turk, who was not badly wounded, and the spoils were declared to be mine.

The French almost mutinied when they heard that my Turk had on him more than four hundred gold sequins. The matter was not helped by the fact that I was the only Spaniard on the galleon, and there were more than a hundred French. Finally, the captain revoked his decision and had the case put to the Señores del Tribunal del Armamento in Malta for arbitration.

This Turkish ship was loaded with soap from Cyprus. A skeleton crew was put aboard her and orders were given to sail her to Malta. As for ourselves, we stayed at sea to look for other such prizes and headed toward the shipping routes of Alexandria in search of them.

† WE FIGHT A TURKISH SHIP †

At sunset, we sighted a ship that seemed very big, as in fact she turned out to be. We followed her wake at full sail so as not to lose her in the darkness. At midnight, we overhauled her and, with our guns loaded and ready, we challenged her.

"Who are you?" shouted the captain.

"Just a ship sailing the high seas," came the reply. And we knew by their insolence that they, too, were ready with their guns. They seemed not in the least frightened. There was, in fact, a good range of artillery and four hundred armed Turks aboard, and their ship was quite our equal in tonnage.

They let us have a broadside. It sent seventeen of our men to the next world and wounded many others. Then we fired a broadside, and it was just as good as theirs. We then went alongside her, boarded her, and started hand-to-hand fighting. It was a hard battle. At one time, the Turks took our forecastle, and it was a long job dislodging them and forcing them back to their own ship. For the rest of the night, we parted company and we stayed in our own ships. By morning, our captain had a plan that proved very good. He battened down all the hatches and only allowed the actual soldiers on deck, where they had either to stay and fight or jump into the sea.

With the dawn, we went alongside the enemy again. The battle was anybody's. We took their forecastle and held it for a goodly time; then they threw us out. We withdrew to our own ship to fight it out with cannon as we were better seamen and could handle our ships better. In this case, we were also stronger in artillery than the Turks.

It was there and on this very day that I saw two miracles that are well worth the telling. And this is the story.

A Dutch gunner was loading his cannon in full view of the

Turks. One of the Turks carefully aimed a cannon at him and fired, and the ball hit the Dutchman squarely in the face. His head was blown to pieces, and the men about him were splattered with the pulp of his brains.

A flying bone from the gunner's head struck a sailor on the nose. From birth, this sailor had had a crooked nose, and in this one blow his nose was made as straight as mine, with only the mark of a bruise to show.

There was another soldier who was so full of misery and who cursed and blasphemed so much that no one in his gun room ever got any sleep. Well, on this day he was hit by a cannonball. It cut across the flesh of his buttocks. After that, no more was ever heard of his misfortunes. The only thing that he ever again said about his life was that he had never known anything like the wind of a bullet to sweat out a sickness!

During the battle we maneuvered our boats into good fighting positions by using our oars. But as night fell, the Turks tried to make for the land, which was not far away. We gave chase and got to the coast at the same time they did.

With the dawn, the sea was calm. It was the feast of Our Lady of the Conception. The captain ordered everybody, even the wounded, to come on deck to prepare themselves to die. Everyone went on deck, I among them. I had had a musket shot in my thigh and had been badly wounded in the head the evening before by a halberd blow when we had boarded the Turkish ship and captured her forecastle. The captain then solemnly said to us, "Gentlemen, prepare yourselves either to dine with Christ tonight, or to wear chains in Constantinople."

We had aboard a Calced Carmelite brother as our chaplain, and the captain then said to him, "Bless us quickly, Father, as this is our last day on earth."

The good father blessed us and, when this had been done, the captain ordered the frigate, which was our store ship, to tow us alongside the enemy. In this way, we were ready to fight, unhampered by the sails and oars.

The battle was big and bloody. We could not relax a moment. Even if we had wanted to break off the engagement, we could not have done so, because the Turks had thrown a heavy anchor onto our deck to stop us from taking to sea. The battle lasted more than three hours. And by that time we knew that we had won, because the Turks had started jumping into the water and swimming for the shore, which was not far away. They had not, however, seen that our frigate was going fishing for them!

We forced our advantage and won the battle. We made prisoners of the Turks who were aboard and clapped them in irons to take back as slaves. We pillaged the ship and did very well for ourselves.

We found over two hundred and fifty dead bodies aboard. The Turks, it seemed, so as not to show the extent of their casualties, had not thrown them into the sea during the battle. So *we* tossed them all in.

On that day, I observed an unusual thing concerning the Christian and Muslim faiths. Listen, and I will tell you.

We had thrown a lot of bodies into the sea when we noticed one floating on its back. Now that was most unusual: Dead Moors and Turks who were thrown into the sea always floated on their bellies with their faces in the water. Christians, on the contrary, floated on their backs.

We asked the Turks we had captured why it was that this body was lying on its back. They replied that they had always suspected that this man was still a Christian. Apparently, he had disavowed his Christian faith long before, but he had once been a Frenchman.

We next put our ship in order as well as the one we had captured. Both, since the battle, were in a bad state. We then made sail for Malta. As there was so much money aboard, and in everyone's pockets, the captain gave the following order, "Until we reach Malta, there is to be no gambling aboard."

And to make certain that we kept our money to ourselves, he

ordered us to throw all our playing cards and dice overboard and published severe penalties for anyone he caught gaming.

So we gambled this way. We drew a circle about the size of the palm of your hand on a table, and in the center of it we drew a circle the size of a silver dollar. Then every player put in this little circle the louse of his choice and bet heavily on it. Each player would follow his own louse carefully, and the first louse to get outside the larger circle won all. And I swear that there was often as much as eighty gold sequins in the pool.

The captain caught us at this, but he realized that, whatever new order he gave, he had no hope of stopping gambling. The vice was too deeply ingrained in soldiers.

At Malta, I went to the law over the slave I had captured at Cape Silidonia. After all the evidence had been heard, the Señores del Tribunal del Armamento announced their decision, which was that the four hundred sequins should go back into the pool to be divided with all the others. However, I was given, as a favor, a hundred ducats, which was the full price of the slave, instead of the ten *escudos* that the captain had offered. Even more important than that, I was granted the right to incorporate the orange and white flag that I had captured in my own heraldic blazon, when I was granted one—a thing I later did with great pleasure.

I gave the flag to the church of Nuestra Señora de la Gracia. My ill-gotten gains from the voyage amounted to more than fifteen hundred ducats, but I quickly ran through the lot.

† WE OUTWIT THE MOORS †

Shortly after that, there were some galleys of the Religion that were sailing for the Levant on some enterprise or other, and I embarked to try my luck.

We made it there and back in twenty-four days. We assaulted a fortress in Morea called Pasaba, and we took five hundred prisoners: men, women, and children. We captured the governor, and his wife and children, as well as horses and about thirty bronze cannons. We did all this without the loss of a single man: The news of it astonished the world.

However, the truth was that the garrison there had thought themselves in no danger of attack, knowing that the main Christian fleet was still at Messina.

Soon after this, in the same year, 1601 [*and it was in that year that Contreras reached the age of nineteen*], the same galleys sailed for the Barbary Coast. I went aboard, as on my last voyage, to see what I could make for myself. We stormed and finally took a town called Hammamet. And this is how we did it.

The evening before the landing, we sighted land. During the night, we approached the shore. Before dawn, the general ordered us to put on turbans and to haul down the foresail so that our ships should be taken for the galliots of Morato Gancho. We hoisted the Turkish colors and lots of gay Turkish pendants and, at dawn, finding ourselves just offshore, played around on deck, as the general had ordered, with drums and flutes just as the Turks did. This ruse succeeded, and we were able to drop our anchors quite near the beach.

The town was very close to where we had moored our ships and almost every man, woman, and child came out to greet us.

Three hundred men, and I was one of them, were detailed for the attack. We landed in a great mob, attacked the gates, and held them. After that, there was nothing more to it; the town was ours.

We rounded up all the women and children and some of the men. Most of the men, however, had fled. We went into the town and sacked it. The loot was mean, but that was to be expected from such miserable people.

We sent aboard seven hundred slaves and this worthless loot. Then three thousand Moors, half on horseback, half on foot, came to the relief of the town. We set the town on fire quickly and wasted no time in getting back aboard ship.

Three knights and five soldiers were killed in this engagement, but they lost their lives only because they were too greedy. We then headed back to Malta feeling pleased enough with the expedition.

At Malta, I frittered away the little that I had earned on this trip. I must explain to you how. There were *quiracas,* as we called them, in Malta, and they were so ravishing and so nimble witted that they made themselves the wives and mistresses of anyone with any money, knight and common soldier alike. It was with them that I spent my money.

† I BLUNT THE ATTACK ON REGGIO †

After I had been a few days in Malta, his highness Grand Master Vignacourt sent for me. He had heard that I was very familiar with the Levant and that I spoke the language well. He gave me orders to go to the Levant to spy out all I could about the Turkish fleet.

I was promoted to sea captain, and my commission was signed and sealed by the grand master. My ship was a frigate with a crew of twenty-seven sailors and soldiers.

I set off and was soon among the Levant islands. I asked news of the Turkish fleet from several ships I met and learned that it had passed through the Dardanelles and dropped anchor at an island called Tenedos. From there, it was going on to the anchorage at Chios.

I tailed the devils until I saw the ships drop anchor at Chios. Now that I knew where they were, I hung around waiting to see whether they would next go to Negropont. Even knowing where they were was really not of much use: I wanted to know what they were going to do. I also wanted to know whether they were going to stay in these seas or whether they were going to attack Christian lands.

I must explain. Every year the general of the sea left Constantinople to visit the islands. Though the islanders were all Greeks, their governors were all Turks. On his rounds, the general of the sea collected his dues and dealt with the year's law cases. Over and above his rents, the islanders, according to their wealth, prepared some fine gift for him. This general of the sea was also the only person who could depose the various governors of the islands.

That year, the general had brought with him from Constantinople the royal galleon and twenty others besides. Included were the Rhodes squadron of nine galleys, the two Cypriot galleys, one of the two Alexandrians, two galleys from Tripoli in Syria, one from Egypt, one from Nauplia in Romania, three from Chios, two more from Negropont, another of the Cavala squadron, and one from Mytelene. Only the galleys of Constantinople and Rhodes belonged directly to the Grand Turk; the others belonged to the various governors of the islands and countries named. Yes, I forgot to add, there were also two from Damietta, a town on the Nile.

I knew that if all these ships did not go to Negropont for careening, scraping, and victualing, it was not probable that they would make for Christian lands. I also knew that when there was going to be an expedition to Christian territories, the galleys of Barbary, Algiers, Bizerta, Tripoli, and any others that were armed joined up with these others in the islands. That was the Turkish way of making up a battle fleet.

This year, they all assembled.

Then I learned for certain that they were all going to Negropont to be careened and victualed.

I sailed round to Cape Maina to wait and spy on them. And from there, after some time, I saw a fleet of fifty-three galleys and several brigantines sailing past on its way to Navarino.

I then made sail for Sapienza, which was an island lying opposite Modon, the fortified town not far from Navarino belonging to the Turks. From there I made for the Venetian port on the very fertile island of Zante.

I stayed there long enough to get news that the Turkish fleet had left Navarino, and to learn with absolute certainty that it was Reggio that the general of the sea was to pillage. His predecessor, Cigala, had done the same. I then sailed to the Venetian island of Cefalonia and, from there, nearly four hundred miles to Calabria.

As soon as I reached the Italian mainland, I went ashore and gave the news of the approach of the Turkish fleet. Plowing up the coast, I spread the news as far as Reggio.

The governor of Reggio, a knight of the Religion called Rotinel, received me well. He quickly made his preparations and massed his knights and his troops, who were then spread around the countryside, as well he might. The Turks were already anchoring off San Giovanni (in the Straits of Messina) only fifteen miles away.

After three days, we got news from the knights who were riding between San Giovanni and Reggio that the Turks had landed their troops.

The governor set an ambush for them and slaughtered three hundred Turks and took sixty prisoners. After this defeat, they reembarked and gave no further trouble.

The governor instructed me to go aboard my frigate, to cross the straits, and to alert Taormina, Syracuse, and Augusta. All these towns were on the Sicilian coast. Taormina, the nearest, was only twenty miles away from San Giovanni. This I did by fighting my way through the middle of the Turkish fleet. I carried out my orders and then went on to Malta to tell them the news.

The knights there immediately prepared to defend themselves. Shortly after my arrival, the Turkish fleet arrived off the isle of Gozo, the well-fortified island that lay next to Malta. They had been warned in good time, so that when the Turks tried to get ashore, our garrison of knights prevented them from landing in force and did not even give them the opportunity of getting fresh water. And that was how the Turkish expedition of that year ended.

† THE CAVE OF THE BLESSED VIRGIN †

I spent a few days with the *quiracas* and then was ordered off to reconnoiter La Cantara. It was a Barbary fortress near the island of Gelves. We had heard that there were two seagoing barges being loaded there with oil for the Levant. So I set my sails for Barbary with my frigate rearmed.

The island of Lampadusa was a halfway house, and it was there that we caught Caradali, the famous corsair. Lampadusa was almost alive with tortoises, and we always used to take a lot of them aboard when we stopped there. There were also thousands of rabbits. The island was as flat as your hand and about eight miles round. The port was big enough to take six galleys. Above the port was a high tower, which was quite deserted. Some said that it was haunted and that this was the island where King Roger and Bradamante fought. But that is just a fable.

However, what was not a fable was that there was, in a cave that was very easy to get at, a painting, on a very old piece of wood, of the Blessed Virgin with the Child in her arms, and this had worked many miracles.

The Blessed Virgin had her altar in this cavern and on it was this picture. On the altar was also a great pile of things that Christians had put there as offerings, such as biscuits, cheese, oil, salted pork, wine, and money.

At the other end of this cave was a tomb. This tomb was said to contain the body of a Turkish marabout, a saint according to their lights. At this grave were also more or less the same offerings as at our altar, and also lots of Turkish clothing . . . but no salt pork.

The reason for this was quite simple. Both Christians and Turks left the necessities of life there so that if a galley slave managed to escape he would find something to eat while waiting for a ship of his own nation. It was the same for Christians and Turks alike. I have seen it at work myself.

This is how the fugitives found out if the ships in the harbor were Christian or Moorish. I have already spoken of the tower: Well, they would go up this tower and scan the sea. When they sighted a ship, they would slip down during the night among the bushes to the port, and by the language they heard spoken aboard it was easy for them to tell whether the ship was one of theirs. If it was, they hailed it and went aboard. Slaves escaped in this way every day. But remember, nobody would dare to take even the value of a pin out of the cave if they were not in dire need. If they did they would not be able to sail out of port. That, too, was well proved.

The lamp on the altar of the Blessed Virgin never went out, by day or night, despite the fact that not a soul lived on the island. Yes, the offerings on the altar of the Blessed Virgin sometimes got too much for the size of the cave, but the Blessed Virgin would not allow any ship of any nation to take anything away, except the galleys of the Religion, which used to take these offerings to the Church of the Annunciation in Trapani.

As I have said, if any other vessel took them, just let it try to leave its moorings and sail out of port!

CHAPTER FOUR

I sailed on all night for Barbary Cape. In the morning, I found myself at the El Seco Sandbank and about ten miles from the shore. There, I saw a galliot with seventeen banks of oars. When she saw us, she hoisted her colors, a huge green flag with three crescent moons on it.

My men began to lose heart when they saw it and the boatswain said, "It's all up. We're as good as slaves already. That is Saïd Mami of Tripoli's ship."

I rebuked him.

"Nonsense," I said, "we shall capture her today. And what a lovely prize she will make!"

I ordered the rowing to be stopped, let the sails flap, and got ready for the fight. I charged my culverin and stuffed it to the muzzle with nails, shot, and sharp stones and said, "Leave it to me, and this galliot is ours. Everyone, on guard with your swords and shields. Soldiers (I had eight Spaniards whom I could trust), load your muskets!"

The Turkish ship did not move herself, but seemed to be waiting for me. Some of my crew wanted to make for the open sea, but I would not think of it. It would have been our complete ruin as I shall explain—to say nothing of my disgrace. So I said, "Friends, do you not see that it is a hundred and twenty miles to Christian land from here, that that ship has extra banks of rowers, and that, in four strokes, she can throw a grappling iron aboard us. In running away, we shall only encourage them. Leave it to me. Damn it, haven't I a life to lose, too? Pay attention now. We shall go alongside as if to board her. Then, we shall let off one volley of our muskets and sheer off. They will lie on their bellies to protect themselves, and as they are getting up I shall slaughter them with my culverin. But leave that last bit to me."

My men understood the plan, and we hoisted our colors. We rushed them, rowing hard, with so much dash that they were amazed. Realizing that we were grimly determined, they struck out to sea, but only when we were nearly on top of them.

I chased them for four hours without being able to catch up. I then ordered the rowing to be left off and the men to have food. The galliot did so, too, and the distance between us remained the same. I again gave chase and they accepted the challenge, until evening when again we both stopped rowing and had food.

I stayed on watch all the evening and all the night to see whether the galliot would take advantage of night to get away, but it became too dark to see. Before dawn, I made the men have a meal, and, to give them heart in case we had to fight, I made an issue of unwatered wine. With first light, I saw the galliot a gunshot away.

I turned my ship toward them and drew alongside them rapidly. Our muskets cracked. They fled at full speed, and we followed. I hung on and drove them until they were forced to seek protection under the guns of the fortress at Gelves.

They jumped overboard into the water, which was only up to their belts, and got ashore. The gunners in the fortress had a few shots at us, but that did not stop me fixing a cable to our prize and towing her out of artillery range.

By way of booty, there were many little things such as muskets, bows and arrows, and clothes. I stripped down the sails and the standard and took them aboard the frigate. As for the ship, I burned her, leaving aboard a lot of junk that I did not want to clutter the frigate with. I then left for La Cantara.

In that port, there was not a single ship, nor were the oil barges still there. Oh, I forgot to tell you where that galliot came from. She was from Santa Maura, an Ionian island and she was on her way to Barbary to be fitted out with cannon for raiding at sea.

From La Cantara, I went to Old Tripoli. I hid in a creek some twelve miles from the town for a day and a night with my masts half hauled down.

The next day, in the morning, a coasting vessel passed. She was loaded with pottery and carried seventeen Moorish men and women. Not one of them escaped me. I made them come aboard my frigate and I sent the coaster to the bottom, but not until I had brought aboard a big earthenware jar full of saffron and some bales of wool.

I went back to Malta and was well received. I was given the price of the slaves; the Religion took them at sixty *escudos* a head, irrespective of their fitness. On top of that, I reaped seven percent of the total value of the loot. I spent it gaily with my friends and my *quiraca,* but most of the money I had earned with so much inconvenience went into her pockets.

† THE BAKE-HOUSE SLAVES ESCAPE †

While I was there, the festa of Saint Gregory was held some six miles out of the town. Everyone went, even the grand master and the *quiracas* too! Scarcely a soul stayed in the city.

I ought to have gone, but I did not, because I was too jealous to allow my *quiraca* out in public. She was very angry with me for not taking her. That day after lunch, while I was making amends, I heard an odd thing: a cannon shot from Castle St. Elmo—then

another. I went down to the street, where I heard someone shouting, "The slaves from the bake house have escaped!"

I ran to Borgo, where my frigate lay, thinking to find my crew
on board. But no, they had gone to the festa, too. I then collected
together a crew of the boatmen who earned their living ferrying
people across the Grand Harbor. I armed my frigate with nothing more than my culverin and some short pikes and sailed out of
port in pursuit of the slaves.

They were getting away in a good bark and had as their flag
a bed sheet. When I got within hailing distance, I shouted,
"Surrender!"

"Come and get us!" the worthless devils replied.

There were twenty-three of them, and they had brought with
them three bows, plenty of arrows, two cutlasses, and more than
thirty spit irons.

"Beware," I shouted, "I am going to sink you! Give yourselves
up and we won't harm you."

The reply came, "No! We'd rather die than be slaves again!"

I let off my culverin, and in one shot I broke the legs of four of
them. As we came alongside the fugitives' boat, they let fly their
arrows and killed one of my sailors and wounded two others. I
went aboard, tied the slaves' hands, and put them aboard my
frigate.

I found that their leader was mauled and on the point of death
from his wounds. So before he took that final step, I hauled him
up a yardarm by one foot and with the man so dangling we sailed
into the harbor.

The whole town was on the ramparts. Even the grand master
had come, hearing the cannon.

The slaves had carried away with them more than twelve thousand ducats' worth of silver and jewels that belonged to their
masters. Only four of these slaves belonged to the bakehouse. It
would have been better if they had all come from there, but the
others were privately owned slaves. I made the best I could of it

for myself and jumped ashore and kissed the grand master's hand. He was very pleased with the service I had done for him and ordered that I should be given two hundred *escudos*. But had I not helped myself to some of the money the slaves had looted, I should not have got a penny for my exploit, because the lords and masters of these slaves accused me of being involved in the escape. One of them even sued me for the price of the slave I had strung up on the yardarm. But they all wasted their time. The slave I hanged was dead and buried, and my *quiraca* in the end was pleased that she had not been to the festa because she got, to her great excitement, all that I had looted from the bark. With that money, she began to have a very grand house built for herself.

† I RESCUE THREE CAPUCHIN MONKS †

A few days later, three Capuchin fathers were on their way from Sicily to Malta on board a ship carrying wood. A brigantine attacked their boat, and they were all taken prisoner. At midnight, when the grand master heard the news, he sent for me; he gave me orders to sail and to lay hands on that brigantine even if I had to go to Barbary to find her.

I obeyed. In Sicily, at Pozzallo Tower, I got word that the ship had sailed for Licata. I went there. There, I was told that she had gone on to Agrigentum. At Agrigentum, they said that she had sailed toward Mazzara. I learned there that she had gone on to Maritimo, which was an island on the way to Barbary where there was a little fort of the king's. There, I was informed that the brigantine had left seven hours before for Barbary. I decided to follow, but my men mutinied and refused to go, saying that there was not enough food.

That was quite true, but I was counting on the Blessed Virgin of Lampadusa, which lay on our course, and on taking victuals

from her and from the marabout. Of course, I had the full
intention of making full repayment. I told my mutinous crew my
plan, and they agreed to sail on.

In the name of Our Lord, I set sail for Barbary. In less than
eight hours, the lookout sighted a ship. I put on more canvas, and
my own strength to the oars to catch her before sundown. We
came up to her fast, neck and neck. The brigantine sheered off to
take cover in an island called Calinosa, hoping to hide in the
darkness of nightfall.

But I beat her. I went for them hard and relentlessly, and when
they hit the shore all the seventeen Moors aboard fled and the
brigantine was mine.

All I found aboard were the three Capuchin fathers, a woman,
a boy of fourteen, and an old man. It was a pitiful sight to see
those Capuchin fathers in irons. I floated the brigantine and put
a guard on her till the morning.

We had food and, in the morning, I sent two reliable men to the
highest point of the island to scan the seas. One was to stay as
lookout and the other to come back with the news. This second
one came back after a while saying that there was not a ship in
sight.

With that good news, I set fire to all four sides of the little wood
in which the Moors had hidden, and soon every single one of the
seventeen came out and I took them prisoner.

I put half of them in my frigate and half in the brigantine.
Half of my men also stayed in the brigantine to keep guard over
the Moors and to sail her. Both ships set sail for Malta, and
received a welcome as they entered the Grand Harbor that I shall
leave to your imagination.

Without mentioning the prize money, this trip made me a sum
of three hundred *escudos*. My *quiraca* had the lot.

In this story, Contreras mentions that the ship that the Capuchin
fathers were on was carrying wood. Today, as much as in those days, it

*would not be at all unusual to see a ship leaving Sicily bound for Malta
with a cargo of wood, water, and plain soil.*

*The knights were not men to be defeated by the barrenness of their
island. They even had a contract with some shipowners for a regular
supply of ice, which was brought from the summit of Mount Etna.*

† I HOLD A TURK TO RANSOM †

Some days later, I was sent to get information in the Levant. I got
ready and left as quickly as possible. I first sighted land at Zante,
six hundred miles from Malta. We sailed among the islands of the
Levant archipelago and anchored off the island of Cerfanto.

Next morning, I came across a little brigantine, which was
careened on one side for cleaning its hull. There were ten Greeks
aboard, and I had them come aboard my frigate. I asked them
where they were going when they had finished sprucing up, and
they replied, "To Chios."

Then I led them into a trap.

"What about the Turks you are carrying?" I asked.

They swore blind that they were carrying no passengers.

"And those Turkish plates on deck? What about them? They
are the sort Turks eat from. And you tell me that you've no
Turkish passengers?"

They stuck to their story.

I started to torture them and not lightly, either. All stood it,
even a boy of fifteen whom I had stripped naked and trussed up.

"Tell me the truth," I said to the boy, "or I shall cut off your
head with this knife."

The boy's father, seeing that I looked determined, threw himself at my feet.

"Captain, don't kill my boy; I will tell you where the Turks are!"
he said.

These were the words of a man whom I had tortured till he had fouled his breeches. Such is the love of fathers for their children. It is a thing to be admired.

I sent some of my soldiers to bring me the Turks. There were two servants and a gentleman. The latter was dressed in a scarlet cloak edged with fur and with gold-damascened daggers on a light chain at his waist. He threw himself at my feet and wiped my boots with his well-trimmed and hennaed beard. I then let the brigantine and the Greeks go on their way.

But I forgot to tell you that my soldiers brought up, at the same time as they brought up the Turks, five of those big coffers—you know the sort, the Turkish ones with curved tops—full of damasks of many colors and a great deal of crimson silk fleece and a few pairs of children's shoes as well.

I then interrogated my Turk, and he answered all my questions. He had just come from Constantinople with a loaded caramousel, and it was because he was frightened of pirates that he had taken passage back in this little brig, which he had thought to be a safer form of transport. And he was quite right, too. He told me that the Turkish fleet was going to the Black Sea, so being thus put at my ease, I opened the subject of ransoms.

"Do you want to buy your freedom?" I asked him.

"Yes," he replied.

After three long discussions, we settled on a ransom of three thousand gold sequins, which his two sons living in Athens were to pay. His home, too, was in Athens.

We sailed there, but I did not want to go right into the harbor, because the entrance was very narrow and it only took twenty musketeers to stop a ship getting out again. I therefore made for a cove about five miles from Athens, where I dropped anchor.

I sent one of the two servants to the city. I gave him only three hours, no more, in which to go and come back. He was on time, and brought the whole nobility of Athens on horseback with him. When I saw so many horsemen, I laid out to sea a little.

They held up a white cloth on a pike, which reassured me, and

I showed my flag of St. John. Three venerable Turks then came aboard and invited me ashore to discuss terms. I talked with one of them, who I gathered, from the respect paid to him, to be their governor. He told me that it was not possible to raise the money till the next day.

"Ah, well," I said, "if that is how things stand, I am on my way."

"You know as well as I do," I went on, "that Negropont is no distance away and that Morato Gancho, the pasha, can easily be told that I'm here and he'll sail here in his twenty-six bank galliot and capture me in no time.

"If you can guarantee me a safe passage by land and sea," I added, "I will stay as long as you like."

"By land, yes, but not by sea," he replied.

"Well, then, please excuse me as I must be off. But remember your Turks aboard my ship."

When he saw that I had firmly made up my mind, he said that he would agree to my terms. He raised his finger in front of everyone and said, "*Hala ylala.*"

This oath was a better guarantee than twenty safe-conducts duly signed and sealed, so I stayed on with confidence. But, for all that, before he had said "*Hala ylala*" he had sent word to Morato Gancho.

As he understood Spanish, we chatted of all sorts of things. He had a young cow killed and cooked, and we sat down and had a meal. In place of our customary wine, we drank a raisin brandy from Corinth. Afterward, they wanted me to go riding with them, but I told them that the only thing I rode was the sea.

Two hundred and fifty of them got on their fine horses, each horse having a colored damask across its back, and they galloped and skirmished. It was a wonderful sight to see.

The ransom money was finally brought and it was in brand-new Segovian silver *reales*. They asked me to accept these, as they had not been able to find enough gold at such short notice. I ordered my boatswain to count them.

He was suspicious when he found brand-new coins so far from

where they had been minted, and he wondered whether they were counterfeit. He came to me and told me his suspicions. I had one of the *reales* cut open. The core was copper, and it was veneered with silver.

I protested. They all swore by Allah they knew nothing of the swindle and, in fact, would have killed the two Venetian merchants who had brought the money on the spot if I had not stopped them. They asked me to be patient long enough for them to send to the town for more. Four Turks then, on four horses, galloped away like the wind.

We were still waiting when Morato Gancho's galliot hove into view at the entrance of the anchorage. When I saw her, I went cold all over, but it all turned out well. In a second, the horsemen were in their saddles and one was waving a white flag on the end of a lance. The galliot steered toward them and dropped anchor where she was instructed, which was about a musket shot from my frigate.

The captain came ashore where the Turks and I were. I went to meet him and we saluted each other—he in his way, I in mine. He wanted to see the man I had captured and requested my leave to do so.

I gave orders that my prisoner should be put ashore with no delay, and gave special instructions that he should be wearing his own scarlet robe and his daggers. This second order was considered a great politeness.

We talked awhile, and the captain asked me to inspect his ship. We rowed out to it, and I was piped aboard. I stayed there a short time, and then we went ashore.

We passed the time pleasantly enough waiting for the money to arrive, which was not long, as the horsemen made the double journey in less than two hours.

They brought the money in golden sequins. In addition to our bargain, they gave me two cotton coverlets, which were as smooth as silk, two cutlasses with carved silver decorations, two bows and two quivers with five hundred arrows glittering with gold dust, and a great deal of bread, brandy, and two heifers.

I had my prisoner's silks and children's shoes put ashore. In gratitude, he embraced me. Then I gave him a present of a piece of his own damask, and I gave another piece to the captain of the galliot. The captain in return gave me some gold-damascened daggers.

Night fell as I was thinking of sailing. The captain asked me to dine with him and to put off my sailing till the morning. I accepted, and it was an extravagant feast. During the meal, the captain received a note from my erstwhile prisoner asking that he negotiate with me for the ransoming of his two servants. He opened the subject straightaway, and I without more ado sent word that the servants were to be delivered to him, saying to the captain, "They are free and under your orders."

This pleased him so much that he wanted to force two hundred sequins on me. But I would not take them. Then he said, pointing to a slave, "Then, have that Christian slave. He is my personal servant and works here in the poop."

"I accept your offer," I replied, "not because I want payment, but so that a Christian may regain his freedom."

I went back aboard my own ship and, in the morning, I asked him permission to put to sea.

"Sail at your leisure," he replied.

I weighed anchor and, sailing up to the galliot, I saluted him with a shot from my culverin. He replied by cannon. We then, each of us, went our own way.

I made through the narrows at Rhodes and anchored at Stampalia, an island with a big Greek population. On this island, there was no Turkish governor but only a Greek nominated by the general of the sea to act as captain general. I was very well known in those islands and much respected by all the people because I never harmed them and used to help them as often and as much as I could.

Whenever I captured some Turkish ship, which I could not get back to Malta, I would make them a present of it and sell them the corn, rice, and flax that these ships usually carried. So well did these islanders know me that when they had some great quarrel among themselves they would say, "Let us wait for Captain Alonso (that is what they called me) and he will settle it for us."

Often they had to wait a year, but when I arrived they would put their case to me and I had to give judgment. And always they submitted to my decision as though it were an order from the Royal Council.

CHAPTER FIVE

I arrived off Stampalia and then sailed into port. It was a feast day of the Greek Orthodox Church.

As soon as the lookouts ashore signaled me and it was known there that I was aboard, almost everybody came out to welcome me, with Captain George (that was what they called their captain general) leading them. They shouted greetings to me, addressing me as "*o morfo pulicarto*," which is to say, "O young hero."

Flocks of married women and young girls arrived at the port dressed in skirts that reached down to their knees and little red blouses with tightly tailored sleeves that opened out at the cuff into deep folds and hung at their sides. They wore colored shoes and stockings. Many of them had on open-toed slippers made of velvet of the same color as their clothes. Those who could afford silk wore it; the others wore scarlet. Instead of wearing their pearls at their neck as our women do, they put them on their foreheads. The richer ladies wore gold earrings and gold bracelets. Among the throng, I saw many of my old cronies, whose children I had held at the font to be baptized.

Everybody was in tears. They cried and beseeched me to right

43

the wrongs done to them. A Christian frigate, it seemed, had kidnapped the *pápaz,* who was their parish priest, and a ransom of two thousand sequins had been demanded.

"Where is he? When was he taken prisoner?" I asked.

"This morning, and we have not heard mass. It is now two o'clock and too late for him to say it," they moaned.

I set myself then to find out what had really happened.

"Where is this Christian frigate that took him?" I asked.

"At Despalmador," I was told.

Despalmador was an island not more than two miles from there. I turned my frigate in that direction and set sail. I was quite justified in attacking Christians, as we were duty bound to fight pirates, Christian or otherwise. These Christians were certainly pirates, sailing without commission, and they were sacrilegious. They robbed Moor and Christian alike, as was plain from their kidnapping the priest and demanding two thousand sequins ransom.

We arrived at the little island in a short time, ready for a fight that never started. I found the frigate. She was wearing a standard with the figure of Our Lady on it. She was a small nine-bank frigate carrying a crew of twenty. I ordered her captain to come aboard, and he did so. I then asked him, "Where was your ship armed and manned?"

"At Messina," he replied.

"And your commission?"

He gave it me willingly enough, but it was counterfeit. So I straightaway embarked half of his men and ordered them to be put in irons. I also put half of my men aboard the other frigate to guard the other half of her crew. Then the prisoners I had taken aboard my frigate started to complain, saying, "It is not our fault. Jácomo Panaro (that was their captain's name) told us that he was sailing under the authority of the viceroy."

"We would gladly serve you," they added, "and follow you to the ends of the earth. As for Jácomo, we are finished with him."

"We did not know," one of them went on, "that he was going to kidnap the *pápaz.* We had no part in it. That is why we didn't take to the sea when you came in sight. The captain wanted to sail away with the priest, but we mutinied and waited for you to capture us."

I changed my mind and did not put them in irons and, instead, put the captain ashore, naked, and with no provisions of any sort. He was to expiate his sin by dying of hunger.

I left with both frigates and arrived at the Stampalia port. All the islanders were there to welcome us. I sent the priest ashore, and these good people acclaimed me and covered me with their blessings.

They soon found out that I had left the captain on the island with no clothes and with nothing to eat. They prayed to me, on their knees, to send a ship to look for him. But I said, "Do not try my patience. I know the way to punish the enemies of Christians and common thieves. You should thank me for not having hanged him."

I left all my men aboard ship and put the frigates under a good guard. Then I went up to the village church with one companion only.

We entered the church; gentlemen sat themselves on the benches—if they had gentlemen in those parts. What I mean to say is that these men were the kind of stuck-up fellows you find more or less in every country.

As for myself, they made me sit all alone on a throne, with a carpet under my feet. A moment later, the priest entered, dressed in his most beautiful vestments, as if for Easter Sunday, and began to chant. The congregation replied giving thanks to God, "*Christo saneste.*"

The *pápaz* censed me and then kissed my cheek. Then, everyone came up to kiss me in their turn, the men first and the women next. There were some very pretty women there whose kisses did not bore me one bit and their kisses compensated for so many of the others which the bearded men had given me. And *what* beards they had!

We left the church to go to the captain's house, where the priest and all the family stayed to dinner. The people of the island took gifts of bread, cooked meat, and huge quantities of fruit to the frigates.

We sat down to the table, where we had a good and generous meal. They wanted me to sit at the head, but I would not; I made the *pápaz* sit there instead of me. The captain's family and his daughter dined with us. His daughter was prettily dressed, beautiful to look on, and a virgin.

We dined and drank to many healths. With dinner finished, I said that I wanted to go back aboard. The priest then got up and very solemnly said, "Captain Alonso, the men and women of this country have closed the gates to make you stay here. They pray and beseech you that you will become their chief and their defender and pledge it by taking this worthy young lady here as your bride. Her father will give you all his possessions, and we will give you ours. We take oath that you will be made captain general by the general of the sea; we shall make certain of that by giving him an especially fine gift and paying our customary taxes promptly. There will be no difficulty; have no fear. And we shall be your devoted slaves. Do not forget, we have sworn it in our church and we cannot go back on our word. For the sake of God, please fulfill this desire of ours, which has been close to all our hearts for so long."

I replied that I could not possibly do as they asked and that I had to go back to Malta to complete the duties that the Religion had charged me with. To do as they wished would bring shame on my name, because people would not say that I had married a Christian on Christian soil but that I had an establishment in Turkey and that I had renounced my faith—I, who value my faith so dearly. Then again, if I abandoned the crew that I had brought with me I would be abandoning them in the heart of Turkey and they would lose heart and *I* should be the cause of their ruin if they should be captured and made slaves.

They saw that my reasons were strong, but wanted me to stay all the same and so they firmly said, "You have got to stay."

I saw that they had plainly made up their minds, so I suggested sending my companion to the frigates to find out what the crews thought of it all. According to the reply I received from them, I said I would decide what to do.

My men went down to the anchorage and told the story. The crews were astounded. But if they loved me up there, down below aboard my ship the men loved me even more. They started to arm themselves. They dismounted the culverins from both frigates and mounted them on a windmill in front of and a little way from the town's main gate. And by my comrade they sent back word saying that they considered that holding me prisoner was a poor recompense for all the good that I had done them. If they did not immediately let me go, they would break down the gate and loot the town.

The islanders were amazed to find that I was so loved by my men and said, "Well, we were not wrong in wanting to keep you as our master. At least promise us to come back when you have done your duty."

I promised them that I would and they asked me to give my hand in token of friendship to the girl and to kiss her lips. I did that wholeheartedly, and I am sure that if I had seduced the pretty thing no one would have minded.

The priest gave me three beautiful carpets as a farewell gift; the girl gave me two pairs of finely embroidered pillows, four handkerchiefs, and two hats worked in silk and gold. They also sent generous supplies of fresh food to my crew and when I said my good-byes they were as miserable as if it were Judgment Day.

† BY THE SKIN OF OUR TEETH †

From Stampalia, I went to an island called Morgon. There, I dismissed the frigate I had captured, but first I made her crew swear that they would never again touch the goods of Christians.

I dismissed them because in those parts it was wiser to travel alone, well armed and with a crew who all slept with one eye open and who understood each other like brothers.

From Morgon, I sheered off towards the isle of St. John of Patmos where the holy evangelist, who was exiled by the Roman emperor, wrote the Apocalypse. On the way, I met a Greek bark that had two Turkish passengers. One, a renegade Christian, was master of the slaves aboard Hassan Marriola's galley. He had just gotten married on an island called Syra. I put them both in irons and let the bark go on its way.

I asked this renegade whether the Turkish fleet was assembled. Being a member of the fleet, it was impossible for him not to know, and he replied, "No."

I went on my way and asked again at Patmos where they said the same. This time I could not doubt its truth because the Patmos ships were always in communication with the whole Levant. There was a fortress at Patmos, which also served as a monastery. The people of Patmos were very rich, and their ships wore the same flag as the ships of the knights of Malta.

I sailed to a small deserted island some fifteen miles distant, called Formacon, with the idea of sharing my booty of damask and money. It was this habit of sharing the booty before arriving in Malta that made me so much loved by my men.

I sent three men ashore to the hills with orders to keep lookout on land as well as out to sea and to send back one man if they saw anything. In the meantime, I ordered the jars of sequins and the damasks to be put ashore. We were getting them ashore when one of the lookouts came rushing down the hill shouting, "Señor Captain, two galleys are nearing the island!"

I quickly had the damasks and the jars put aboard and ordered the sails to be hoisted and the booms lashed at such an angle that the sails caught no wind.

Then the other two lookouts came down and said, "Señor, we are already as good as slaves."

I ordered all hands on deck, weighed anchor, and waited. I was ready to sail at a second's notice.

I was in a creek and the galleys were sailing together, so I assumed that they had not then seen me. If they had seen me, they would have approached me on each side of the island and met at the creek, so that if I had tried to escape they would have been sure of catching me.

One of the galleys appeared at the head of the creek. She was going at full speed and did not notice me until she had gone quite a way past. When she saw my frigate, she swung round and the other galley followed suit. Then the two of them dropped their sails and rowed toward me with a great deal of shouting.

One galley came right up to me, so that my poop touched her prow. The captain, brandishing a cutlass, got on the bulwarks but, for fear of being pushed overboard by his riotous crew, stopped any of his men from making me go aboard or even passing me a cable.

I saw that by ill discipline and bad seamanship both of the galleys were in wild disorder and when the tumult reached its height, I saw my chance to escape. I let go the rope in my hand, the boom swung out and my sail filled. We put some distance between ourselves and the galleys, and then I had the other sail hauled up.

Both of the galleys were equally crippled by having dropped their sails down on the long bridge which ran from poop to prow above the rowers, and by the time they had got them up again, caught the wind, and were after me, I was more than a mile away.

Quickly, though, they came out of the creek and sailed to seaward of me, so that to make the open sea, I had to cross their bows. Then the wind dropped and I had no hope of being able to do so. They chased me for eight turns of the hourglass without gaining a foot. The wind blew again, and I raised canvas. They, too, hoisted, and they gained on me. Their artillery opened up: One shot hit us and carried away the standard on the mainmast.

Another shot hit my rigging. The mainyard tumbled, and I was frightened that we should be sunk and even more worried when I saw the enemy's captain use an old sailor's trick. Everyone on board had crowded to the prow to take a look at my frigate and by their weight they were slowing the speed of the galley. But the captain set up a barricade in the middle of the ship and ordered his crew to stay astern of it. This made the bows of the galley lighter; she bucked and gained on me foot by foot.

I saw that all was nearly up for us, so I put my wits to work. The position was very simply that if I could not get across their bows to the open sea, I was sure to be run aground before long.

But there was in those parts, just offshore, an island called Samos. There was a sort of harbor there, which the Maltese galleys used to hide in before pouncing on their prey. I steered toward this island and sent a sailor up the mast with a bowl of gunpowder. I ordered him to make two smoke signals and to wave his hat in the direction of the island.

Seeing me do this, the Turks thought there must be some galleys of the Religion at anchor there. They dropped their sails, changed course, reset them, and fled with such speed that in a short time they had vanished from sight. I then made for Nicaria Island, where I felt safe as there were some good high lookout posts.

The next night, I sailed for Micono, where I came across a French coaster, loaded with goats' skins, coming from Chios.

Her captain told me a story about a captain with two galleys he had met who said that he had chased a frigate. This captain had nearly died of grief at having let the frigate slip between his fingers. The captain, he told me, was Soliman of Gatanea, the man who had once been a Genoese butcher.

When I said to the Frenchman, "That frigate was mine," he was so excited that he could not stop talking about it. He warned me that Soliman had gone to wait in ambush for me as I left the archipelago. So I decided to make direct for Malta. I waited for a good north wind, set sail, and was soon out of danger.

I arrived at Malta, and everyone was astonished at the story I had to tell. We then divided the money and the damasks, but in doing so put enough aside to make a present to the church of Nuestra Señora de la Gracia. Our gift was a set of vestments for high mass, a chasuble and two dalmatics. And believe me, after a voyage like ours, it was a thanks offering most willingly given.

The whole of Malta was very happy to know for certain that there would be no Turkish expedition that year.

† A BAD BARGAIN WITH THE MOORS †

A few days later, I was sent out again. I was given two fine frigates, one belonging to the grand master, the other to Commander Monreal, my old master. This was only a looting expedition. I was not asked to get any information.

I sailed from Malta with these two frigates. Both of them had thirty-seven men aboard, and each ship looked as impressive as a galley. I steered toward North Africa and first sighted land at Cape Bonandrea, a run of some seven hundred miles. I coasted along the salt flats until I came to Port Soliman, where I stopped to take on fresh water. Here, I was unlucky as a large number of Moors were then passing that way on a pilgrimage to Mecca to visit the tomb of Muhammad.

They laid an ambush for me at a well to which I was sending for water. Around this well was a wall of rushes. And since the Moors were naked and brown skinned, my men did not see them hidden among the rushes.

Twenty-seven sailors with barrels were working, with sixteen soldiers with muskets to protect them, when the Moors attacked. The sailors left their barrels and ran, leaving the soldiers to cover their retreat with musket fire. When I heard the sound of firing, I landed with twenty more soldiers.

The Moors had already nearly driven my men back to the

beach when they saw help coming. Then they stopped. They had captured three soldiers and had killed five, a loss which I could ill afford. We took two of them: an old man of sixty and another scarcely any younger.

We showed a white flag and bargained for the release of our soldiers. I offered them an exchange of two for two and a price for my third.

"No, no," they replied, "you've got to buy back all three. You can keep the two Moors."

There the matter rested until they called again saying, "How much will you give us for your barrels full of water?"

"I don't need water," I replied, "but I do want my Christians back."

But the truth was that I needed the water much more than the men, as I only had two more jars aboard. If they did not let us have our barrels, we were well and truly lost. So I said to them lightly, "How much do you want for each barrel?"

"A golden sequin," came the reply.

Asking was one thing, giving another. We had almost no money at all aboard, as we had only just left port and had captured nothing. So I replied, "We have no gold aboard."

"Then give us biscuits," they replied.

"Agreed," I shouted. I then gave them a shieldful of biscuits for each barrel. This suited me very well, as I had plenty of biscuits.

I recovered all twenty-seven barrels and then opened up negotiations for swapping the two Moors for my two Christians, but they were adamant.

As night was falling, I buried the dead on the beach and put a cross at the head of each grave. I then told the Moors I would be back in the morning.

In the morning, I was horrified to find the bodies I had buried lying exposed on the seashore. I thought that they must have been dug up by wolves. But when I got nearer, my spirit chilled. I saw that each body had lost its ears and nose and every heart had been torn out. I thought I would go out of my mind at the sight. I showed a white flag and when they had come near I tried to explain to them what a foul thing they had done.

"We are taking these bits and pieces," they replied, "as a thanks offering to Muhammad."

When I learned that my three live soldiers had been butchered, too, I angrily swore that I would cut my own Moorish prisoners up in the same way.

"Do as you like," they replied. "We think much more highly of ten sequins than thirty Moors."

Then in their presence I cut off the ears and noses of their prisoners and threw them on the ground in front of them, shouting, "Take these to your Muhammad, too!"

We went back aboard, taking the two Moors. I tied them back to back and in full view of those ashore I threw them into the sea.

† I CAPTURE A CARAMOUSEL †

I then sailed toward Alexandria.

I found nothing on the coast, so I decided to go to Damietta, which was on the Nile Delta. I went up the Nile to see what I could find but met nothing. I turned back and crossed over in the direction of Syria, a distance of 130 miles. I sighted the shores of the Holy Land, which were only some thirty-five miles from Jerusalem. I passed on and entered the harbor of Jaffa. There were a few barks there, whose crews all fled ashore at my approach. From there, I went along the coast to Castel Pelegrin, and from there to Haifa.

On a little point on one side of the harbor, there was a hermitage, a musket shot or less from the sea. It was said that the Blessed Virgin Mary rested there during her flight to Egypt.

I carried on to the port of St. John of Acre. I found some ships there, but they were too big for me to take on, so I had to go on to Beirut.

I called at Surras on the way. The two cities there belonged to the emir of Surras, a Turkish prince who was so powerful that he did not even acknowledge the supremacy of the Grand Turk. One of his brothers had been to Malta once, and he had been feasted, honored, and finally sent home with a thousand presents from the Religion. For that reason, all the ships of the Religion could take shelter in that port and were always generously welcomed. If any Christian prince got it into his head to do a pilgrimage to the Holy City, it was most helpful to have the use of this port and the friendship of people who could put thirty thousand men, mostly cavalry, into the field if protection were needed.

I sailed into the harbor. The emir was away, but when the governor saw that I was of the Religion, he welcomed me just as warmly and sent aboard a free supply of fresh provisions.

I sailed on toward Tripoli in Syria—a fine city. I stood out to sea, when I came abreast of it, so as not to look an easy prey for the two galleys which I saw in the port. I then made for Tortosa Island, which was close to the Galilee coast. It was a flat little island and covered with flowers the whole year round. There was a legend that Our Lady and St. Joseph hid from Herod there, but I would not vouch for its truth. We scraped our ship's bottom and lived well on the young pigeons there. There were millions of them; they made their nests in the holes of the ancient water cisterns.

It went without saying that I kept a very good lookout in those dangerous waters. One day, the lookouts informed me that a ship had been sighted coming toward us, so I went to have a look myself and recognized her as a Turkish caramousel.

I rallied my men and waited. When she came abreast of the island, I went out to meet her. She fought well, as all Turkish ships did, but was beaten in the end. They had thirteen dead and I, five—four sailors and a soldier. I captured twenty-eight, some fit and some wounded, and among them a Jewish peddler with a store of junk. The ship, however, had a cargo of linen and Cyprus soap.

I put all the men from my supporting frigate aboard the caramousel and instructed them to tow their frigate and sail straight back to Malta. I had not enough men to keep both frigates fully armed as well as man the caramousel; in that way, I kept at least my own ship in good fighting trim.

From Tortosa, I went up the coast to Alexandretta, the place where we sacked the warehouses. From there, we sailed along the Caramanian coast to Rhodes. Our route was as follows. We went from Alexandretta to Bayas and from there to the Langue de Bagaja. From there, we traveled on to Escollo Provenzal, Port Caballero, Estanamur, Satalia, Port Genca, Port Venice, Cape Silidonia, and Finica, where there was a good fortress. After that, we went to Port Caracol, El Cacamo, Castilrojo, Seven Capes, Aguas Frías, Lamagra, and finally to Rhodes. I sailed next on to Scarpanto Isle and then toward Crete.

While making for Crete, I got caught in a *burrasca* squall, which drove me for two days and two nights back north into the Levant archipelago. I first hit land at Iali, where the story ran that the body of either St. Cosmas or St. Damian was found. The Greeks there sold me fresh victuals, and as soon as I had them stowed aboard I set off for Stampalia, the place where they had wanted me to marry and settle down. When I got there, everyone came down to meet me, thinking that I had come to keep my promise.

I did not dare land! I told them that I had come with the galleys of the Religion and that I had made this trip just to see them and to ask if they needed anything and that I had to rejoin the fleet at Paros immediately.

They were very disappointed, but they all sent aboard gifts of fresh food. They told me also that after my last visit they had gone in a bark to look for Captain Jácomo Panaro. They brought him back and entertained him until the arrival of a French schooner that had come from Alexandria. They next put him aboard with a store of food and ten sequins for his expenses and instructions that he was to be taken to Christian lands.

† I WHIP AND SALT A MAINOTEE †

I took leave of them and again set off for Malta. In the Gulf of Nauplia in Romania, I fell on a caramousel loaded with corn and a crew of seven Turks and six Greeks. The Greeks swore that the corn was theirs but under torture changed their minds. So I put the Greeks ashore and made for the Maina promontory, which was quite near.

This part of Morea was very bare, and the inhabitants were Greek Christians. Although they were Christians, one would not think so from the way they behaved. They had no proper homes but lived in caves and were renowned robbers. They had no elected chief; they obeyed only the strongest man of the tribe. Despite the fact that Maina was in the heart of Turkish territory, the Turks had not tamed these people. Not only had they not subdued them, these hill men used to rob the Turks of their cattle!

They were very fine archers. I saw one day a man wager to shoot an orange off his son's head at twenty paces. He shot it off with such nonchalance that I was amazed.

Their shields were made of leather and were elongated rather than round. Their swords were broad and often more than four feet long. They were also formidable runners and swimmers. Also, they liked to be baptized four or five times, or, for that matter, as many times as they could find anyone to do it. The reason for this was that godfathers, according to their custom, were expected to give them some fine present. So every time I passed these shores I always baptized a few!

I got to Port Quoalla on the Maina coast with my caramousel of corn. Immediately, an old crony of mine called Antonaque, who was then chief of the Mainotees, came aboard. He was well dressed and wearing damascened daggers with thin silver chains. At his side he had a cutlass with a silver-mounted hilt.

He came up to me and embraced me. I ordered a drink to be served him as was the custom and told him that I was towing a caramousel of corn. I asked him if he was interested in buying it. He said he was, and we settled for eight hundred sequins and the boat. In fact, the boat by itself was worth more. He asked me to wait until the next day to give him time to collect so much money.

At midnight, these bandits cut the caramousel's anchor cables and dragged her ashore.

By the time I saw what they had done, there was nothing I could do about it. At dawn, we visited the ship on the beach to see what was left, but these brigands had worked so hard during the night that there was scarcely any corn left aboard her.

Soon after, my crony, with two of his friends, came aboard and said, "Please excuse me. None of this was my doing. You know as well as I what sort of people these Mainotees are."

I pretended not to care at all about the loss of the ship and ordered breakfast to be served for the four of us. But while we were having breakfast, I had the anchor weighed and we sailed out of harbor.

"My friend, put me ashore," he pleaded.

"I'm only on a little reconnaissance voyage," I replied.

But once out of the harbor, I said, "Breeches down, my friend!"

"This is treachery," he wailed.

"Yes, but you have done worse to me. Come along now, less talk and breeches down! Consider yourself fortunate if I don't hang you from the yardarm."

He stripped himself naked and four of my strong boys pinned him down and gave him more than a hundred strokes with a rope end dipped in tar. Then, as was the custom in the galleys, I had him washed in salt and vinegar. While he was undergoing this treatment, I said to him, "Send for my eight hundred sequins or you hang."

He saw that I was not just having a joke at his expense and immediately ordered one of his men ashore. I did not want to go back to the harbor, so this man threw himself into the water and swam ashore. In an hour or even less, he came back bringing the eight hundred sequins in a goat's skin. I dismissed them all and the three of them dived into the sea and swam home. From that day on, in Malta and in the archipelago, I have been jokingly called "the Mainotees' friend."

I set sail for Sapienza, and from there took the high seas to Malta, where I arrived in five days. Everyone was pleased to see me again. The soap and the slaves that I had sent ahead in the caramousel, along with my supporting frigate, had already been sold. I divided the spoils between the two crews and I did well out of it. My *quiraca* was able to go on with the building of her house. On top of the first spoils, our crew alone divided the eight hundred sequins and the seven slaves which we had brought.

† I GO TO BUY SOME PEARS †

We had a good time for a few days, but soon I was instructed to rearm the frigate and to prepare for sea; but I was not told where I was to go.

This is how it was. News had come that the Turks were equipping a huge squadron and no one knew where it was aiming to attack. There was a great deal of concern about it in Malta. To put an end to their worrying and prepare themselves for the worst, the knights, who were by no means fools, thought up an excellent plan.

When the Grand Turk prepared an expedition, the Jews had to make an interest-free loan. When the fleet was to stay in Turkish waters, the sum was so much; when it was to go outside Turkish waters, the sum demanded was more.

The collector for the Constantinople and Caramania districts used to live in Salonica. We knew that he was living at that time with his family in a fortified house some five miles from the town.

My lords, the knights, told me to go and get him. It was just as if they had asked me to go down to the market and buy some pears!

They gave me a spy and a bomb. I took my leave and, with my trust in God, reached Salonica. But I did have trouble, as Salonica was in the middle of Turkey and one had first to go through the archipelago.

Sixteen men and I jumped ashore with our bomb and our spy—I did not trust that spy an inch—and we got to the collector's house, which was about a mile from the sea. I laid the bomb, fired it, and it did its work well. We went in and took the Jew, his wife, his two little daughters, a houseboy, and an old woman. All the men of the house took to their heels.

Without even allowing my prisoners time to put on a coat or my men to steal an inch of cloth, I ordered everyone back immediately to the beach. Despite all the speed with which I had carried out this operation, just as we were getting aboard four hundred horsemen galloped into the water up to their horses' necks and there yelled abuse at me. But they were too late, and we got aboard safely.

The horsemen swung round and started careering round the countryside, while I fired five-pound cannonballs at them.

The Jew offered me anything I asked for if only I would release him. But I would not risk it, though I could easily have done so because I quickly learned from him what I had come all that way to discover. The Turkish expedition was to be directed against the Venetians and the Grand Turk was going to demand a million sequins from them with the threat that if they did not pay he would capture Crete, which was a Venetian island, and as long as Sicily, and lay in Turkish waters.

I consoled the Jew by telling him that we were going to Malta and not to Venice, where he would have had a hard time of it. On my course, I met a Greek bark and I asked them where they had come from.

"From Despalmadores in Chios," they replied.

"Are there any galleys there?" I asked.

"No," they replied, "Soliman of Catania, the bey of Chios, has sailed in his galley *La Bastarda* and left his wife in his summer pavilion at Despalmadores."

Then my pilot said, "By God, we must capture her and carry her off to Malta! I know the house as though it were my own. And now Soliman is away, we shall find the place unguarded."

Having the company that I had aboard, I was not willing to chance it. But my pilot tempted me so much, assuring me that it would be easy, that in the end we did it. And it proved even easier than the pilot had promised.

We waited for nightfall and, at midnight, we went ashore, ten of us and the pilot. The pilot went straight up to the house as though he owned it, knocked on the door and talked about Soliman being expected back any minute. The door was opened for us and we all went in. Without the slightest violence, we picked up the renegade wife of Soliman. She was a Hungarian and the most beautiful woman I had ever set eyes on. We then laid our hands on Soliman's two *putillo* boys, a renegade and two Christian slaves, one a Corsican, the other Albanian. We looted a bed and all the clothes we could find without anyone making a murmur of complaint.

We went back to the ship and sailed as fast as we possibly could until we got out of the archipelago and God granted us a favorable wind.

The Hungarian was not the legitimate wife but only the concubine of Soliman. But I treated her with great courtesy. I learned later that Soliman, thinking that I had slept with her, condemned me in my absence and swore to search me out and have me outraged by six negroes and then impaled.

But he did not have the good luck to catch me, even though he finally had portraits of me made and put up in various Levant and Barbary ports. He wanted people to recognize me and send me on to him, should I fall into their hands.

These portraits were made in Malta and were taken away by the Turks who had come to bargain for the ransom of the Hungarian concubine and the harem boys. This happened the next year when Soliman became king of Algiers.

I arrived in Malta and was received as well as you might imagine, especially as everyone could relax when they heard my news. The Italian infantry, which had been raised in Naples and Rome and was on its way, was sent back.

My pilot was not so fortunate. In less than four months, while he was raiding in a schooner, the Turks took him. They skinned him alive and stuffed his skin with straw and put it on the main gate of the city of Rhodes, where it can still be seen.

He was a Greek, born at Rhodes, and the most capable pilot who ever sailed those seas.

† THE GRAND MASTER EMBRACES ME †

While I was in Malta squandering my money, which had been earned the hard way, I surprised my *quiraca* in bed with a friend of mine. Imagine, being in bed with my acquaintance while I was being good enough to build her a house! Well, she ran away and hid.

I ran my sword through him twice and left him for dead. But he recovered and, before he was mended, fled from Malta fearing that I would kill him.

Though everybody begged me, men and women alike, to take her back, I could not see why I should. Especially as I was then able to take my pick of the other *quiracas*, who were fighting over me as though I were some vacant post in the government.

I stayed in Malta, without leaving once, for many months; it was a miracle. Then, at last, I was sent to Barbary with a frigate. I went and returned in nine days, bringing back a coaster loaded with enough fine cotton to open a shop, and fourteen slaves as well. It was, for me, a very profitable voyage.

In the days that followed, a Catalan galleon arrived. It was on its way from Alexandria to Spain and was loaded with all sorts of luxuries. This ship reminded me of my country, and I thought of my mother to whom I had never written and who had had no news of me. I decided to ask the grand master for permission to go home. He agreed, though he did not wish to lose me. And when the time came for our farewells, he put his arms around me and laid his cheek against mine.

CHAPTER SIX

I went aboard this galleon, the *St. John,* and in six days we arrived in Barcelona.

There I learned that the court had moved up to Valladolid and that new promotions to the rank of captain were being made. Because this meant that new infantry companies were being raised, I made all speed to Valladolid without going first to Madrid.

I presented my papers at the Council of War. One of the councillors was Don Diego Brochero, who later became the grand prior of the Order of St. John of Jerusalem in Castille and Leon. He took to me—he already knew all about me—and asked if I wanted to be a lieutenant in one of the many companies that were being raised. I said that I would, and the next day when I went to see him he said to me, "Go kiss the hands of Captain Don Pedro Xaraba del Castillo for the honor he has done you in trusting you with his standard."

I presented a memorandum to the Council of War asking them

to approve my new post. This they did, taking into consideration the modest services I had done for my country.

I then bought two drums, one for each of the drummer boys who had enlisted with me, and an impressive flag. The captain gave me my commission and the right to raise my flag in the town of Ecija and in the Marquisate of Pliego.

I got mules and, with a sergeant, my two drummer boys, and my personal servant, we set off for Madrid. We arrived there in four days.

My first stop was at my mother's house. When she saw so many mules at the door, she did not know what to think. Then I went up to her and knelt down and asked for her blessing, saying, "I am your son Alonsillo."

The poor woman could not believe her eyes and was frightened because she had married again. She felt as guilty about having done so, as if she had committed some fearful crime, and she was terrified that her grown-up son, and a soldier, too, would not approve. But, after all, for one who had already had so many children, it made no difference.

I comforted her and told her not to worry about it. Then I excused myself and went to take rooms at the inn, as there was no room in my mother's house. It was small even for them.

The next day, I decked myself out in my smartest military dress. With my soldiers looking their best and my servant behind me carrying my lance, I went to pay my respects to my stepfather. They invited me to dine with them that day—heaven only knew if they had enough for themselves—so I sent them all the food that they would need for the meal.

With the dessert, I called for my two little sisters. I gave them some toys, which I had brought from abroad, and cloth for some dresses and for suits for my three little brothers. As I was not poor, there was something for everybody. I also gave my mother thirty *escudos,* and with them the good lady thought herself rich! I again asked her blessing and the next day departed for Ecija, recommending her to respect her new husband.

† WE CATCH SOME ROBBERS AT ECIJA †

I arrived in Ecija and presented my commission to the councillors who were then in session. They gave me permission to fly my flag on the Palma Tower. The drums rolled, I made the customary proclamation, and set about enlisting soldiers. This did not prove too difficult, as the sheriff and the gentlemen of the town were kind enough to give me their support.

When men enrolled, they immediately picked up the military habit of gambling. It was also a custom in the army that the drummer boy kept a terra-cotta jar for the pool, and, in the evening, he would break the jar open and with the proceeds the soldiers would buy dinner.

Our guardroom was at the bottom of the Palma Tower, and it had a wrought-iron grill looking onto the street. One day, four roughs called in at the guardroom. They had been in before but had never done any harm. However, this time they broke open the earthenware money jar and counted out the money at their leisure. It came to twenty-seven *reales*. One of them pocketed the lot and said to the drummer boy, who was the only one of my men present, "Tell your lieutenant that some of his friends had great need of this money."

The little drummer boy rushed to call the corporal, but when they had both returned the men had gone. The little drummer then came to find me to make his report.

"Go back to the guardroom," I said to him, "and make your report to me there."

When I arrived there he said to me, "Sir, Acuna, Amador, and some others came in here. They broke the money box and took twenty-seven *reales* from it. They then said to me, 'Tell your lieutenant that some friends of his needed it.'"

"You silly little fool!" I replied. "Does it matter that these gentlemen have taken some money away? Any time they come, let them have what they ask for, just as if I myself were asking you. If they take the money, you can be sure it is because they badly need it."

I said this because I knew that there were many of their friends listening and that they would tell the robbers straightaway. I learned later that they had said among themselves, "What a frightened little mouse that lieutenant is!"

I then set about planning some suitable way of punishing this insult to myself and to my troops. I bought four muskets and kept them in an armory close by the guardroom. I already had twelve short pikes there. A few days passed, and these robbers took courage again and went into the guardroom.

I had enrolled 120 soldiers (it was true that 100 of them were billeted out in the Marquisate of Pliego). However, I had twenty with me, all veterans, whom I was personally maintaining and paying.

Well, when the robbers went into the guardroom, they had no suspicion that I was waiting for them. I ordered my men to get their muskets, light their firing tapers, and enter the room behind me. For musketeers, I had chosen only my most reliable men and had ordered them to fire at the first sign of resistance. I had the rest of my men stand by the door with their pikes. With a lance in hand, I went in and said, "Drop your weapons, you low thieves!"

They couldn't believe that it was not some joke, but when they saw that I was in earnest they grabbed for the hilts of their swords. My musketeers then stepped forward ready to fire and shouted, "Surrender!"

They then gave up their swords. I stripped them down to their breeches and led them away with ropes round their necks like dogs and handed them over to Don Fabian de Monroy, the sheriff. He was delighted to see them. When he had looked them over, he said, "That's the one who killed my watchdog, and this one here murdered my servant."

The whole lot of them were put in prison, and within two weeks those two were hanged.

I kept their capes, their swords, jerkins, stockings, garters, hats, and two of their embroidered waistcoats as well as such money as they had with them. With it, I fed and clothed some of my poor soldiers. So I got repayment for the twenty-seven *reales* in the end.

† I FIND I HAVE COMPANY †

Soon after, I learned that there were some men pretending to be soldiers, roving the countryside, begging in the name of charity from the peasants and robbing them.

I took my four musketeers and a well-behaved mule and went to search them out. I got wind that they were at Cordova, so I went there. At Cordova, I found Captain Molina raising another company of infantry.

I stopped at Las Rejas Inn and then went alone to the local brothel street to have a look and to see if I could track down these thieves there. I had already learned what these men looked like.

While I was talking with one of the many girls there, a gentleman, but not one carrying any badge or staff of office, came up to me with his servant and said, "Where have you got that jerkin?" (It was made of cowhide.)

"On my back," I retorted facetiously.

"Well, take it off," he said.

"I have no wish to," I replied.

His servant then said, "Then I'll make you."

He started to try to do so, and I had to draw my sword. They were not slow to do the same, but I was quicker. I wounded the gentleman, whom I soon discovered to be the senior policeman of the town and an unscrupulous rogue in the bargain.

Hearing the fight, the women of this cul-de-sac locked their house doors and the big door which closed the street from the rest of the town. I found myself master of this very narrow street when I went out, but I had no idea what to do. It was the first time I had been in quite that sort of brothel street. So I went up to the gate at the end of the road. But it was securely locked. There was not a soul to speak to or anyone I could ask for the key. Everyone had carried or followed the police officer and his servant into one of the houses where he was presumably well known.

Then I heard someone knocking on the gate. A little urchin popped up from nowhere and opened it and there was the town's sheriff and as many men as you may well guess behind him. They were all ready to attack me, so I threatened them with my sword saying, "Forbear, gentlemen!"

It was all the same, if there had been one assailant or one thousand, because they could only come through the door one at a time. Meanwhile they were shouting, "Seize him!"

But no one fancied the risk of going through the gate. There would certainly have been some ugly incident if Captain Molina had not come with the sheriff. He recognized me and said, "All right, lieutenant, all right. Sheathe your sword."

I recognized him as soon as he spoke, and I replied, "All right, but first make these gentlemen sheathe theirs; I am only defending my skin."

The sheriff, hearing me referred to as lieutenant, asked, "Where does this lieutenant come from?"

Molina replied, "From a company he is raising in Ecija."

"But what right has he to come here killing the elders of the law?"

I then came forward and personally explained all that had happened. I tried to justify myself further by explaining that I had only come there in search of robbers. But he ordered me back to Ecija that very day all the same, and I said that I would obey. In the end, I took my leave of the sheriff and went away with the captain and his men.

I went back to the inn and, while I was packing my bags to leave the town, one of my four soldiers came to me and said, "There are two gentlemen below who are asking to speak to you."

I went down and said to them, "What can I do for you, gentlemen?"

One of them replied, "You, sir, you are the lieutenant?"

"Yes," I replied, "and what do you want of me?"

With a great show of twirling his moustaches, one of these gentlemen slowly set himself to explain: "It is as salutary to know men of goodwill—such as your grace—as it is to serve them. We have been sent by a good lady, whose husband was unfortunately hanged at Granada on the false witness of perjurers. She is a widow with no responsibilities, and well set up in life. She admires your grace and begs you to join her for dinner this evening."

This was so much Greek to me and I could not make head or tail of it, so I said, "Gentlemen, would you be kind enough to tell me what this lady sees to admire in me to be worth this honor?"

"Is it not enough to have fought like a giant and wounded our chief of police, who is incidentally the worst robber in Cordova?" they replied.

Then I guessed that the lady was one of the girls in the brothel. So I said to them that I much appreciated the favor but that I was due to be made a captain shortly and that I could not risk losing my promotion by not obeying the orders to leave town immediately. I added that I wished that it could be otherwise.

After that, I took leave of them and rode back through the night to Ecija. I looked in at the guardroom and found all quiet. There had been no troubles while I had been away, which was good news to me.

Three days later a soldier came to me and said, "Sir, at the Sun Tavern there is a woman who is asking for you. She has come from other parts and she's not bad looking, either."

I went to the inn, as any young man would [*Contreras was twenty-one at the time*] and met this lady. The innkeeper had given her his private room. She appeared to me to be a good-looking young woman and when I asked her where she came from she replied, "From Granada."

Then she went on to tell me that she had run away from her

husband and that she had come to me for protection. She begged me to hide her away somewhere.

It seemed a good idea to me, so I took her into my house and entertained her, all the time keeping her hidden from public view. I was beginning to fall in love with her, when one day she said to me, "There is something I must tell you, but I have not the courage."

I pressed her to tell me. And, having made me promise that I would not be angry with her, she began: "Sir, I first saw your Grace in a house in Cordova. You were so brave and so strong that day that I had to run after you. Oh, how easily you wounded that robbing police officer! When you would not come and dine with me, not even when I sent the most respectable men to invite you, I was even more determined to follow you." She paused, and then went on, "Since I was left alone, after the hanging of my man in Granada, many famous men have sought me out, but of all these fine gentlemen, none was as worthy as yourself to sleep at my side."

She then pointed out quite clearly that in the whole of Andalusia, no woman was a better investment than herself: If I doubted her word, she told me to ask the "madame" of the Ecija brothel.

I was flabbergasted with her story and, as I had grown fond of her, I could really see nothing wrong in what she had done. In fact, it seemed to me that she had paid me a pretty compliment in coming to seek me out.

Then, on top of all this, the commissariat captain came to review the men, to give us our marching orders, and our stores. I summoned all the men I had in Pliego Marquisate and in all I lined up 193 on parade.

We took the road through Estremadura for Lisbon with light hearts. I took my woman with me with the confidence that no one could possibly guess that she was a lady of easy virtue rather than a colonel's daughter. She was young, beautiful, and no fool; everyone treated her with respect.

CHAPTER SEVEN

My captain had gone home from the court and waited there until he had heard that the company was on the march. He joined us at Llerena and was very pleased to see so fine a company. He said that he was astonished that I had known how to discipline recruits so well. We stayed good friends in proportion to the amount of flattery I gave him.

On the next night's stop, we received orders not to enter Portugal but to occupy ourselves in Estremadura Province. We marched from village to village for a while and finally arrived at a place called Hornachos, where, with the exception of the priest, everyone was Morisco.

Being a Morisco did not necessarily mean that one was an African Moor who had turned Christian. The great majority of the Moriscos of Spain were of the same race as the Spanish Christians, but their forefathers had become Muslims during the Moorish and Arab domination of Spain between the tenth and thirteenth centuries. Subsequently, their descendants had become Christian again.

In 1525, the Muhammadan faith was made illegal and from 1609

71

even Moriscos were expelled from Spain. Any connection, however distant, with the infidel was suspect—and not entirely without cause.

It is estimated that between 120,000 and 300,000 Moriscos were expelled, with the majority going to the African mainland, where large numbers were slaughtered by the Moors. The disruption of this large section of the community is often considered the reason for the decline of Spain's power.

Contreras's story about the arms shows how deeply the Spanish government was worried about the Moriscos, but it does not explain why the commissariat captain did what he did.

I settled myself in the house of one of these no-goods, and flew my flag on it. I made the same house serve as the guardroom as well. That evening a soldier named Vilches came to me and said, "Sir, I've made a find."

"How's that?" I asked.

"I'm living in a house," he explained, "where I haven't been able to get a proper bite of food because the people say they have only got jam and figs in the house. I looked round the house hoping to find some chickens and, in a room at the far end of the house, I found the round cover of a corn cellar. I scraped round it and found that it moved. I hauled it up and everything was dark below. Hoping that there would be some chickens, I lit a candle, which I had with me, and went down the ladder which I found already there in place. When I got to the bottom, I was almost sorry I ever started. Against the walls there were three tombs, much whitewashed, as, in fact, was the whole cellar. I think there must be some Moors buried there. If your grace would like to go there, and if these are tombs, we are sure to reap some jewels for our trouble as Moors are always buried with their gems."

"Let us go," I said.

I took my lance and we two went alone to the house. We went in and asked the woman of the house for a candle. She was frightened at seeing me, for her husband was not at home, but she gave us one. We went down the corn cellar and, when I saw the graves, I agreed wholly with the soldier. They looked like Moorish tombs.

I dug the blade of my lance in one of them to lever up its top. In a moment, a plank, which was under the plaster top, gave. I discovered that the tomb was a large coffer, made of wood but decorated with plaster so as to look like a tomb. And it was full of muskets and shot!

I was delighted. I saw myself arming the whole company with them and our being more respected on our marches. Up to then, we were only armed with short pikes, some of the men not even having those, and we had lost face in more than one town.

I opened the other tombs and in each was the same. I said to the soldier, "Stay here until I find the commissariat captain and report it to him."

I went to find him immediately and told him all about it. He followed me with his bodyguard and his secretary. When he saw what was in the tomb, he said to me, "You have done a fine service to the king; now go back to your lodgings. Not a word to anyone about this; it is a serious matter. Now not a word, remember."

He gave the same instructions to the soldier, who came back to my lodgings with me. When we got there he said, "Sir, I still haven't had any dinner this evening."

I gave him eight *reales* to go to the inn and he was as happy as Christmas Day. I wanted to report all this to my captain, but in the end I did not tell him—first because I had been bound to secrecy and secondly because we were not getting on well together as he was after my woman.

Very early the next morning, the captain sent the drummer boys to me with orders to march. I could not understand why, as we were to have stayed at Hornachos three days. Still, I obeyed and left.

As we were about to start off, the commissariat captain said to me, "God be with you." Then he added, "Those Moriscos, by the way, had royal permission to hold those arms, so don't think about it again. But if they hadn't had permission there would have been a fine ado. Anyhow, let it be, and say nothing about it."

We left for Palomas, stayed there two days, and then went on to a village called Guarena, where the men had a quarrel with the villagers. It ended in a brawl with three dead and a few wounded on both sides.

During the fight, the soldiers were shouting, "God's blood! If we only had some of those muskets from the Hornachos cellar!" My soldier had already told his companions about them, and I myself had spoken about them more than four times.

The quarrel settled down and we moved on. The commissariat captain arrived there a few days later to punish the villagers for setting on us. This captain was a regular officer. I will not tell you his name for his sake, but you will see later in this story what a stir these tombs full of arms raised. But let us leave that until its proper place.

† ISABEL FALLS OFF A DONKEY †

My captain at that time was lusting after the woman I had with me. He had let her know this quite clearly by all sorts of signs and messages, but he had gotten no response from her. She had grown wise after all the promiscuity of her past.

We arrived at Almendralejo and as night fell I billeted the company. I had dinner with my woman and then sent her off to an early bed as she was three months with child. Then the captain sent for me and said, "Take eight men, go up the Alange road, and wait in ambush there. I have had reliable information that four soldiers are intending to desert tonight on that route."

I believed him, had my pony saddled, and started off, leaving my woman in bed asleep.

When the captain heard that I had left, he went to my lodging to pay a visit to Isabel de Royas—that was her name. One thing led to another, and finally he wanted to get in bed with her.

She defended herself bravely and cried out for help. The captain grabbed a mallet of the sort used in a game called *mallo*—a delightful game, by the way—to silence her. He attacked her so savagely that the owner of the house and the men on guard were compelled to come in and drag him off her. By then, she was in such a state that she was seized with a flux and aborted within three hours.

All this time, I was in the countryside, aware of nothing that was happening, watching for my fugitives. When I saw it was only two hours before dawn, I said, "Let us get back, men. This joke has gone on long enough; that is if it is a joke the captain has played on me. Anyhow, these men would have fled earlier in the night than this if they were going to do it at all."

I returned to my lodging. When I got to my room I found Isabel groaning with pain. I asked her what had happened, and she said, "I fell off a donkey last night so hard that I had a flux and, worse, I miscarried."

I noticed several soldiers, who were at the door, whispering to each other while she was saying this. It made me suspicious, so I pressed her to tell me the true story. But I could not drag another word from her. I went out of the room and called to me a soldier whom I trusted and asked him what had happened.

"Sir," he replied, "such brutality has been committed here that I cannot keep quiet about it. The captain came here and got Señora Isabel in this condition, just because she was a modest woman. By God, I swear that all of my companions and I will have deserted before nightfall. We left our homes for you, sir, and not for this disgraceful captain, whom we know nothing about."

"Calm yourself," I said. "Whatever the captain has done, Señora Isabel must have done something to deserve it."

"No, as long as God lives, no! It was because she would not let him get in bed with her that he attacked her."

The facts seemed plain enough, so I ordered my pony to be fed and packed a bag with some money and my papers. I went along to the captain's lodging. His Flemish servant Claudio answered the door and said that his master was asleep and that he could not wake him at such an hour. I told him that a courier had come from Madrid and only then was the servant willing to awaken his master. After a few moments, the captain shouted to me, "Wait a minute."

He got half-dressed and asked me to come in. I went in with my sword in my hand and said, "You're a low sort of gentleman to have done what you did last night. I'm going to kill you for it."

He made a reach for his sword and shield, but justice was stronger. I lunged my sword into his chest and he fell to the ground, moaning that he was dead.

His servant tried to come to help him, but he did not succeed. In the little scuffle I had with him, I sliced a chunk of flesh out of his fat head.

I mounted my pony and took the road for Cacares. I had some friends there, knights of St. John, and I told them the whole story. Then next day, they sent news to the commissariat captain, who arrived at Almendralejo in no time. Later, I learned that he held an inquiry there and that he had condemned me to be executed on the charge of having attempted to kill my captain in his own quarters.

One must remember that one can do nothing worse in the army than show lack of respect for one's superior officers.

The findings of the inquiry and the sentence were sent to Madrid. However, it was all in my favor, except that I had not been obedient to my superior officer, who, though he had been perilously near death, eventually recovered from his wounds.

I wrote to Don Diego Brochero, who was a knight of the Order of St. John, and he told me to come to the court, adding that he would see the affair through all right for me. So, on the advice of the knights at Cacares, I went to Madrid.

The council at Almendralejo gave Isabel, after her convalescence, the wherewithal to go to Badajoz to think out what was best for her. (I must explain that she had been without news of me for many days.) In this town, she opened shop in a bawdy house, and of all the brothels in Estremadura it was not the worst.

I arrived in Madrid and stayed with Don Diego Brochero. He had been at the conference at the Council of War and he told me that all the councillors were on my side.

He ordered me to present myself formally at the city prison, where I would write a memorandum to the council making myself their prisoner. I would beg them to look into my case. I subsequently awaited their decision and swore that what I had done was in no way connected with the king's service.

My making myself a prisoner before I put up my memorandum was thought very well of, and materially helped my defense. Then out of the blue I was given a dispatch to take to Don Cristobal de Mora, viceroy and captain general of Portugal. I did not know what it contained, but Don Diego Brochero said to me, "Go on your way happy. You are carrying good news." But, for all his encouraging words, I left feeling thoroughly scared.

The companies were then still held up in Estremadura Province, but I did not meet them as I took a different route to Lisbon after Almendralejo. I passed many of the places which I had been through before and was given a good welcome as I had a name for trying to do good and never ill to the people I met.

I got to Almendralejo, where the two magistrates of the town welcomed me like some lost brother. I told them that I was carrying a dispatch from the king, and I inquired after Isabel. They told me that they had sent her off to Badajoz, where she had wanted to go when she was well. They said how sorry they were about the whole incident. They told me that the day after, half the men had deserted. I later learned that the captain had at that hour only 20 soldiers left out of his 150 or more. The captain made his ceremonial entrance into Lisbon with no more than fourteen men and a drummer boy; that I know as I made that entrance with him.

I said farewell to the magistrates and went straight on to Bada-joz to find Isabel, for I still loved her. I found her earning her living in the brothel. When she saw me, she got up abruptly, closed the door and said, "Welcome, sir. But a word first, I pray you; please come with me." She led me into the "madame's" part of the house and started to weep.

"Why are you crying?" I asked her.

"Because I am so happy to see you," she said, "and although you see me here, I swear I have not slept with a man since you left me."

The madame backed her up, saying, "You can believe her. And I will be her witness. Four gentlemen of this town have showered presents on me to make me give Isabel to them, but I have not been able to make her agree." The madame paused. "She was certainly a wise girl to keep the respect of a fine man like your grace."

"I kiss your hand," I replied, "for the compliment."

Isabel and I then set about deciding what next to do.

"I have six hundred *reales* and some nice things to set up house with. What would you like to do?" she asked.

"Since I am compelled to go on to Lisbon, let us both go," I suggested, and we agreed to do that. That evening I went to an inn and Isabel came to dine and sleep with me.

There were some men in that town who wanted to sleep with Isabel and as they had been unsuccessful they were determined to give whoever succeeded a bad time. So they brought the sheriff to my inn during the night to arrest me and turn me out of the town. They had told him I was the most double-dyed ruffian in the whole of Spain.

To cut the story short, they broke in on us in the middle of the night, and since there is always a great difference between a naked man and one with his clothes on, the sheriff took advantage of me and started to manhandle me as though I were a criminal. He ordered me off to prison. I got dressed and, when I had done so, said, "Señor, do not insult people until you know who they are."

I then told him who I was, and that I was carrying a dispatch for the Council of War. He knew my name already because of the Almendralejo scandal and I told him that this was the woman who had been attacked by the captain.

He was delighted to make my acquaintance when he learned who I was. He begged my pardon a thousand times, and complained that he had been quite led astray by the false allegations these men had made against me.

He asked me to stay inside the inn and to move on to Lisbon as soon as I conveniently could. He added that if I needed anything I had only to tell him and he would see that I got it. I thanked him and he went his way and I mine, back to bed. I stayed in the town two more days and everyone stared at me as though I were some prize bull.

I did not let Isabel go back to her brothel for anything. I had the master of the house bring all her goods and chattels. He did so but with a heavy heart at the thought of losing a pearl of such price forever.

We went on to Lisbon in easy stages and waited there for the infantry companies to arrive. After twenty days, mine arrived along with four others. They had come down the river from Alcantara. Before they disembarked I delivered my dispatch to Don Cristobal de Mora, the viceroy and captain general of Portugal. He was very polite and said to me, "Go down to the river, when the troops disembark, join your company and make the ceremonial entrance into the city with them."

I pointed out that the captain was likely to create a scene as I had not seen him since I had wounded him. Don Cristobal then sent his adjutant to take a message to him, informing him that I was to rejoin the company. The captain replied that he wanted to see Don Cristobal about it. He came, and Don Cristobal said, "Be patient. You have been given the king's orders, but in a few days from now you will no longer have Contreras with you."

We landed our standard, which had been put aboard ship at Alcantara, and marched to the castle. We were reviewed and promptly disbanded, with the result that the captain and I parted company forever.

Don Cristobal de Mora gave me a month's pay and permission to go to the court. With God's help, I went my way. At Valladolid, I was offered eight *escudos* over and above my pay to serve in Sicily. I accepted it and went on alone. Isabel came with me as far as Valladolid, where I left her. There, later, she died doing that thing at which she was most proficient. May God forgive her.

I went to Madrid to see my mother and to ask her blessing. That done, I set off for Barcelona and went aboard a ship loaded with flags bound for Palermo. In ten days I got there and joined an infantry company commanded by Don Alonso Sánchez de Figuero.

In that year, 1604, the duke of Feria was governor of the kingdom of Sicily. The duke wanted at that time to equip some galleons for raiding and knowing that I was well broken in to seafaring ways, invited me to command a ship. I accepted his offer.

I sailed for the Levant and I captured for the duke a flat-bottomed Egyptian riverboat, bursting with all the good things of the world. We captured it at Alexandria. I also took a little English galleon that had been raiding for three years; she was full of most strange objects. All the other things that happened on this cruise I will leave out, so as not to bore you with too many stories of the Levant.

With what I made out of this voyage I bought a stableful of horses—I was dripping with money—and I moved in the society of the Marquis of Villalba, the eldest son of the duke.

CHAPTER EIGHT

Preparations were in hand for an expedition to Barbary with Sicilian and Maltese galleys. Four were from Malta and six from Sicily. They were all under the orders of Adelantado of Castille, the general of the squadron.

He lost his life, and I shall tell you how.

We sailed for Barbary in the ten galleys. Adelantado ordered the men from the Sicilian squadron to leave their breastplates and chain-mail coats at Messina so that they should be able to fight more agilely.

We got to Zembra, an island eight miles off the Barbary mainland. A council of war was held, and it was decided that the troops should land at Hammamet. Hammamet was the town that we had captured several years before with the Maltese galleys.

In the small hours on the eve of the Assumption in 1605, we landed our men six miles from Hammamet. We marched across the sand dunes and arrived there an hour after sunrise. I was one of seven lieutenants in charge of scaling ladders. We were a squadron of five hundred men, everyone a Spaniard, and each with either a javelin or a musket, but wearing no breastplate.

We laid the ladders against the city walls and held them firm. And, as was usual with such Spanish soldiers and knights of Malta, we scaled them courageously, some toppling off, but the others always onward and up.

Briefly, we took the walls, cut off the heads of the guards in the ravelins, and found some janissaries among the garrison troops.

The town gate was opened and our troops poured in. Another squadron, the one from Malta that must have numbered seven hundred, stood guard outside the town. We could scarcely move in the narrow streets since the streets were less than nine feet wide, and there were so many of us.

We captured some Moors and their women, but very few. The rest of them had hidden in the corn stores that one finds under every Moorish house.

Outside the walls, there were some vegetable gardens watered by waterwheels, where there were a few Moors on foot and others on horseback. I believe that there were fifteen on horse and about a hundred on foot, but they were kept in check by the Maltese squadron there.

Then the trumpet sounded the retreat. We left the ladders against the walls and that made our defeat total, as I shall explain. No one knew who had blown the retreat. But everyone gathered up the bits of loot he had found and ran back to the seashore to embark. The galleys by then had approached the town and were only a cannon shot from the beach. Without further orders, the men started to get into some of the longboats that were near the shore. When Adelantado heard of what was happening, he exclaimed, "Who on earth gave this order?"

And no one knew.

Nothing could stop the troops' retreat. Then the Maltese squadron, which had been outside the town, did the same. Seeing the others running off to embark, they broke ranks and fled to the beach with not a single Moor chasing them. This resulted in the whole army of twelve hundred men finding themselves together at the water's edge.

Then the Moors in the vegetable gardens mounted the ladders we had left behind. These were lying against the wall on the landward side of the town. The Moors had not noticed that one of the town gates was open on the other side.

Then the Moors who had hidden in their corn cellars came out and, together with the others, peppered us from the town walls with their artillery. We had not spiked their guns, nor even dismounted them.

But if God ordained that this should happen, how could we be expected to keep our heads? And we certainly lost them that day.

On top of all these calamities a storm sprang up. What was more, even this storm was against us, as it blew off the sea onto the land so hard that all the galleys thought they were going to be wrecked on the beach.

The horsemen who were in the gardens and some men on foot attacked us on the land. The butchery was unbelievable. Not a soul resisted them. We were almost all there, about twelve hundred of us, and they were scarcely a hundred. They had no muskets but just lances, scimitars, and short wooden clubs.

This was surely manifestly a miracle and a chastisement for us ordered by God, and God is just.

Some of those on the beach with me threw themselves into the water; others threw themselves face down on the sand. The rout was so frantic that I saw a small boat on the beach in which thirty or even more men were sitting, believing themselves safe as long as they were in a boat, even if it was not in the sea.

All those who did not know how to swim drowned. As for myself, I stood fully dressed in the sea, with the water up to my chest. Under my clothes, I had on a coat of mail, worth fifty *escudos* and weighing twenty pounds, which I had borrowed from the boatswain of my galley. He always brought it with him from Sicily on these expeditions. I should have had the sense to throw it off and swim out to the galley. To do that was dangerous enough, even though I swam like a fish, but I was so distraught that I could not think of anything. I stood there, stupid, staring at six worthless Moors cutting the heads off all the men sitting in the boat and not one of them showing any fight.

After that, the Moors threw all the dead bodies into the sea and launched the boat. They then milled around killing all those they found swimming. They had no interest in taking prisoners. During all this, we were bombarded by cannon and musket fire from the town.

In the galleys, the sailors were detailed to take the longboats to the beach and pick up as many of our men as possible. But they dared not go inshore, as the storm was blowing hard and they were frightened of being grounded on the beach and being slaughtered.

It happened that one of the longboats had for its master the owner of the mail coat I was wearing. He recognized me by my purple cap edged with gold and my purple jacket. "Strike out to sea," he shouted at me, "we'll pick you up."

This I did without taking off any clothes. A complete lunacy! I swam a couple of strokes and, what with the burden I was trying to carry and the force of the storm, I started to sink.

The boatswain, not wanting to lose his chain mail, bore down on me, grabbed me by one arm, and hauled me aboard. I had about a gallon of seawater inside. There was a poor devil of a soldier, half-drowned, who was holding onto the longboat and dragging it with the waves toward the beach. The boatswain cut his wrist through to make him let go. He drowned immediately. It made me very sad to see such a thing happen, but there was nothing else to do if the longboat was to be saved.

As for myself, the boatswain took me aboard the galley, where, head down and feet in air, I was made to sick up all the seawater I had swallowed.

Meanwhile, Adelantado, seeing how badly things were going, went to board his own felucca. He had left this ship under the orders of a friend, an infantry officer. But when this captain had seen the disaster and felt the force of the storm, he fled.

The story goes that Adelantado shouted for him, crying his name and calling, "Comrade!" I will not say his name, because of the infamous thing he did, namely, deserting this noble lord.

Adelantado had tried to swim but quickly succumbed. A long-boat from the flagship recognized him and dragged him aboard, but it was too late as he was already dead.

Adelantado was taken aboard the flagship of the Sicilian squadron. I saw him laid out on an old carpet in the poop, dressed as he was ashore, but with his face black and swollen. I thought then how little difference there was between being a grandee or a poor soldier. General as he was, Adelantado had not been able to save himself where lesser men had succeeded. Of all the Sicilian regiment, there were only seventy-two men left alive and we were eight hundred when we first set sail. The Maltese galleys suffered just as badly, though I never heard the number of their casualties.

I said that I had seen Adelantado aboard the flagship: this was how it came about. Aboard my galley, myself and six men were all that were left of the company; all the other officers were lost. So the ship's captain sent me to visit the galleys to see if I could find any more of our company alive. I took the longboat. By then, God's wrath had been appeased by so many deaths including that of Adelantado, and the sea was flat and as white as milk.

We had captured a country and lost it: All that, and with a storm thrown in, had happened in less than three hours.

I went aboard the flagship. There were no other soldiers there except the captain of the felucca. All the others had gone ashore and never returned. It was then that I saw General Adelantado as I described before in this story. I went back to my galley, which was then weighing anchor.

It was remarkable how in this short time the beach had become as peaceful as if this butchery had never happened. The Moors had killed almost every man they laid hands on. Some escaped by hiding in some big local-made jars—rather like Spanish wine jars—which were leaning against the landward postern gate of the town. But there were less than thirty men who escaped in that way.

The Moors took our colonel, a knight of the Order of Calatrava, Don Andrés de Silva by name, alive. They debated between themselves as to whom he belonged and finally, while he was still alive, cut him in half, so that both parties should have a share. When we heard what had happened, our hearts bled for him.

The Moors cut off all the heads from the dead and buried their bodies. They decked out everyone of those they had taken alive with a necklace of heads and a pike with a head impaled on it. And in this grotesque glory they made their triumphal entry into Tunis. So ended our disastrous adventure.

We sailed for Sicily and, on the way, the galleys of Malta parted company with us and made for Valetta.

We sailed into Palermo Harbor, with our masthead lanterns draped in mourning. With our awnings up, as it was August, we rowed out of time, looking a pathetic sight. The more dejected we looked, the more the boats came out to meet us asking after a husband or a son, or some for a friend. But we could only keep answering the truth, "They are dead. They are dead!"

The women wailed so much that even the galley slaves wept.

During the night, the body of General Adelantado was taken ashore and carried in a great torchlight procession to a church, the name of which I have forgotten, where it stayed until it was taken to Spain. Proceedings were taken against the captain, who had abandoned the general by taking away his felucca. This captain's brother, an important man in Palermo, seeing that his brother would be condemned to a sordid and shameful death, one night gave him poison. The captain was found dead and swollen like a wineskin the next morning. As I have already said, I will not tell you his name, as he was very well known.

† I MARRY A WIDOW FROM MADRID †

My company was put back on a war footing, and I was sent to live in Monreal, some four miles from Palermo. My host was a baker, and he kindly lent me, for my daily ride into Palermo on duty, his fat ambling old mare.

At that time I was a handsome and colorful young man, and many people were jealous of me. However, on the road that I traveled on every day to Palermo, there lived a Spanish woman from Madrid. She had come to Sicily with her husband, who had been a judge; at the time I met her, she was a widow. She was beautiful and by no means poor. Every time I passed her house, I saw her at the window and I concluded that she had ideas about me, so I found out who she was and sent her a note.

"May I serve your grace in any way?" the message said. "I, too, am from Madrid and feel it my duty, rather than anyone else's, to assist a lady from my own city."

She sent me her thanks and invited me to visit her. I accepted her invitation, took her a present of fruit—Monreal fruit being the best in Sicily—and showered her with compliments.

One thing led to another, and we talked lightly of love and marriage. For her part, being married to a judge, and a learned one, was a very different thing from being wed to a soldier with four lace collars and twelve *escudos'* pay. However, when she started talking seriously of marriage, I said to her, "Señora, I could not keep up a carriage for you, nor as many servants as you now have, though you are worthy of many more."

"All that doesn't matter," she replied, "I shall be quite content with a litter, two maidservants and two menservants."

That being the case, we asked the archbishop for permission to marry secretly at a hermitage. He gave it us, although this annoyed the duke of Feria when he heard. He had been told by the duke of Arcos that my wife would have made a most suitable wife for himself.

We were happily married for eighteen months, and we loved each other very dearly. How I respected that woman! Often, even out of doors, I would not wear my hat in her presence.

And this is how it all ended. I had a friend, whom I would have trusted with my own life, who came and went in my house as freely as I did. Despite this friendship, he set his eyes on my beloved wife. Though I noticed his manner had changed, I did not dream that he was interested in my beloved. Then one day a little page boy of mine came to me and said, "Señor, do ladies in Spain kiss their husband's relatives?"

"Why do you ask that?" I asked.

"Because your cousin has kissed madam, and madam has shown him her garters."

"Of course it is a custom in Spain," I replied, "otherwise my cousin would not have done such a thing. However, don't tell a soul and if you see it happen again, tell me, and I will speak to them about it."

The boy came and told me of a second time that it happened. I could get no sleep for worrying about it, but I did not show it on my face until one morning, as fate would have it, I found them in each other's arms.

They died.

Let us hope that at that sad moment they were repentant and that God will have them in his heaven.

There were many other things that I could tell you about all this, but even this much is an unpleasant memory for me. I will not even mention their names.

However, I took none of her money, not a penny. It was all given to the son she had had by her first marriage.

And so with my papers of service in my bag, I went my way.

CHAPTER NINE

I went to Spain to see about a promotion. The year was 1608. It was suggested to me by the Ministry of War that I should accept the rank of captain and the post of sergeant major of Sardinia, which had then fallen vacant. This post was given me after the Council of War had approved it, but Don Roderigo Calderón— God rest his soul—wishing to get me out of the way and to get the post for the brother of one of his men-at-arms had the following put on my commission: "Only with the approval of the governor of the captain general of Sardinia."

A notice like that was an unheard-of thing to find on a writ. I told the secretary, Francisco Gasol, so. He just shrugged his shoulders. I then took a mule and set out for the Escurial to speak to our king, Don Philip III, about it. He told me to go to see Don Roderigo Calderón, who was at the time also at the Escurial.

"But, sir," I replied, "it was Roderigo who wrote this on my papers."

This irritated him, and he dismissed me saying, "All right, all right: I shall have this looked into immediately."

I went back to speak to Don Roderigo, but he already knew

what had passed between the king and myself and said, "What makes you think that it was me who added those words to your papers? Get along home."

I left, but an hour later two men came up to me and said, "Would your grace be so kind as to come with us?"

It seemed to me as though I was to be taken to some court of law, though neither of the men had any badge or sign of office. But after what had happened with both the king and Roderigo, I concluded that there was going to be some sort of justice dispensed—and I was right. The men led me off between them, talking and asking me questions about what I was petitioning from the king.

In this way, we arrived at the village below the Escurial. I started to think that they were taking me to the jail, which was on that road, but no, we passed it by.

Once we were about two musket shots out of the village, the man on my right put his hand under his cloak . . . but I was watching him. Without allowing him a moment's advantage, I drew my sword and struck him on the head with the flat so hard that he fell to the ground. I then saw a court lawyer's briefcase in his hand, which had been hidden by his cloak. If it had not been for that, I should have run him through. The other man, who turned out to be a police officer, drew his sword, too. I dodged his thrust and drew a line on the ground with the point of my sword saying, "If you cross that line I'll cut you to pieces."

The police officer then set about staunching the blood that was flowing from the other man's head. This done, they informed me that I must never again enter the Escurial without the king's permission. If I did, I did so at the risk of my neck.

"And what about my mule at the inn?" I asked. "Can I go and get that?"

"No," they said, "we shall send it to you."

Quickly, they bandaged the man's wound, making him look presentable, and hurried back to make their report.

I heard that the king laughed a great deal over the affair at dinner that night.

A peasant brought me my mule, and I rode off toward Madrid. But on the journey I came to accounts with my conscience and made a determined resolution. This resolution was that I would serve God in the desert, as a hermit, and that I should quit the court and the palace forever.

† I BECOME A HERMIT †

I entered Madrid with my determination unshaken and went to my lodgings, where I went ahead with the preparations for my last journey. I intended to go to Moncayo and to build a hermitage on that mountain and to finish my days there.

I bought the things a hermit needs, such as a hair shirt, a whip of chains, and other scourges, some coarse cloth to make a habit, a sundial, plenty of penitential books, a skull, some seeds, and a little hoe.

I packed the lot up in a big bag and took for my journey two mules and a mule boy. I left without telling anyone where I was going. I dismissed my servant, and my mother blessed me. She thought that I was going to take up the post of sergeant major in Sardinia, as did many other people who saw me pass by the church of San Felipe and take the road for Alcalá de Henares and Saragossa.

At the Arcos gate, there was a customs search. When they asked me to open my bag, I said, "I beg of you not to open it. There is nothing in it which is dutiable. In any case, what can you expect a soldier, who has just come from the court, to have?"

But they insisted. They opened it and took out all my hermit's equipment and were almost dumbfounded.

"Señor, where are you going with these things?" they asked.

"I am going to serve another king, for I am weary of this world," I said.

When they saw the sort of things that I was taking they were very sorry for me, and my mule boy could not control his tears and cried like a baby.

The mule boy and I passed on from there, talking of my retreat. At Calatayud, there lived some knights of Malta who were friends of mine. I called on them to ask for letters of introduction to offer to the bishop of Tarazona, as Moncayo was in his diocese.

These knights tried to dissuade me from taking up so hard a profession. They knew my past and what sort of a man I was. But when they found that they could not make me change my mind, they immediately gave me all the letters that I needed. But at the same time they also wrote to the bishop beseeching him to use all his powers to make me turn back. This bishop was a religious of the Order of St. Jerome, and he had been King Philip II's confessor.

When I got to Tarazona, I settled myself in an inn. I then gave my mule boy leave to return home with his mules, but the boy had grown so fond of me that he was loath to leave.

After two days, I went to see the bishop and to submit my letters of introduction. He had me stay to dinner and afterwards preached me a little sermon, pointing out the thousand difficulties and inconveniences to which I was in danger of exposing myself and the particular problems such a life held for a young man. [*Contreras was then twenty-six.*] But he could not shake my resolve.

I stayed with him for a week and was entertained well in his house. I had sermons all day and every day, until he saw that he had no hope of altering my course. Finally, he gave me a letter to the vicar of Agreda, which was a town in the foothills of Moncayo. I made my way there and presented my letter to the vicar. He marveled at my determination and told me that I could start being a hermit as soon as I liked.

The sheriff of Agreda was an old friend of mine from Madrid.

He asked me to come and stay with him and, for a little while, turned my thoughts to other things.

However when my intentions were known by the whole town and it was seen that I had the sheriff as my advisor (he had the reputation of being a man of the world), I had everybody's support. When they saw that I really was going through with my plans, they helped me build my hermitage.

I sited it at a spot some two miles from the town, on the slope of the mountain. I furnished it with a statue of Our Lady of Grace and, for the rest, only the barest necessities. I made my general confession at the Franciscan monastery of San Diego, which was just outside the town on the road to my hermitage. The parish priest came to bless my hermitage on the day I first put on my habit. He said a mass there, and my friend, the sheriff, and many of the gentlemen of the town were there.

When the mass was over, they all went back to the town, leaving me on my own. I then set about organizing my life and preparing a timetable of the various occupations that would be good for my soul.

My hermit's dress was the habit of the Franciscan brothers, and I wore no shoes or stockings. I used to come every morning to hear mass at the monastery, and the monks always tried to make me join them. But I did not want to.

Every Saturday, I would go into the town to beg for alms. I would never accept money. I only begged for oil, bread, and garlic, which were the foods upon which I lived. I used to eat three times a week a soup of garlic, oil, and bread, all cooked up together. For the rest of the time, I lived on bread and water and such herbs as I picked up on the mountains.

I went to confession and received the sacrament every Sunday. I took for my name as a religious Brother Alonso of the Mother of God. On certain days, the monks made me eat with them to encourage me to join their order. When, however, they at last realized that I would never become a Franciscan, they put pressure on me to leave off wearing the Franciscan habit.

The outcome of this was that I had to leave it off—a thing which I did not want to do. I then took the habit of the Victorine Order. And if there had been any Victorines in that part of the country, I really think that I would have had the same trouble. It was just a case of monks wanting a hermit to join their order.

I led this life for nearly seven months and no one heard ill spoken of me. I was as happy as if life were one long Christmas Day. And I promise you that if I had not been dragged away from there and if I had been allowed to stay there until today, I would have been working miracles.

† KING OF THE MOORS †

But let us go back to the time that I was at Hornachos. Five years had passed since 1603 when I took to my hermitage and retired from the world in 1608.

There was a rumor in Spain that there was going to be a rising of the Moriscos. Don Gregorio López Madera, magistrate of Casa y Corte, went to Hornachos to hold an inquiry into a rebellion that some Moriscos were accused of plotting. At Hornachos, he hanged six Moriscos. I do not know for what reason. Let it suffice that he hanged six Moriscos. But I do know well that some peasants from Guarena came to Hornachos to sell their "whatever-peasants-sell" and saw these Moriscos strung up. "So there was something to it when those soldiers," the peasants said, "passed through here a few years ago saying that these heathen had a cellarful of arms."

The magistrate had asked the peasants if they remembered who the commander of the company was, but they did not know. He then sent a man into Hornachos and into all the surrounding villages that had had soldiers billeted in them, to find out all he could. This was an easy assignment, as when troops were billeted the captain had to issue a signed proclamation.

My captain's name was soon found out. He was known to be in Naples at that time. Then someone volunteered this information, "There was a lieutenant, and it was his fault. He found the cache and, instead of distributing the arms, went away without telling a soul."

The magistrate then set about finding who this lieutenant was. No one in Hornachos knew, so he sent a letter to the court asking who was the lieutenant to Captain Don Pedro Xaraba del Castillo in 1603. It did not take them long to discover that it was me.

The magistrate tracked me down. He learned that I had not taken up the post in Sardinia and that I had become a hermit at Moncayo because I had written to my mother and to my friends in the secretary of state's office. (The secretary of state was then Don Andrés de Prada, the elder, and a man who had been a good friend to me.)

A royal warrant was dispatched ordering my arrest. The law suspected that no one except me knew precisely where these arms were and also thought it odd that I should have refused the post in Sardinia at a time when the Moriscos were hunting for arms. What was worse my retirement as a hermit to Moncayo was suspect, too, because Moncayo was one of the most easily defensible places in Spain and was in communication with Aragon and Castille, bordering both. They did not know my reasons for withdrawing from the world and could only conclude that I was king of the Moors.

Señor Llerena, a court police officer, arrived with a warrant at Agreda. He secretly visited my friend, the sheriff of Agreda, and they collected a posse of men and set off for my hermitage.

As the road to my hermitage was scarcely a royal carriageway— it was really no road at all—I was surprised to see such a crowd of armed men. I assumed that they were a band of recruits on their way to Aragon. But when they took the path to my hermitage, I did not know what to think. As they closed in on me, they spread out in military formation.

They came toward me. I waited patiently, a rosary in one hand, a staff in the other. They seized me, quickly strapping my hands behind my back and clamping my legs in irons. They then seated me on a donkey, tied me down, and took the road back to the town. During the journey, I heard someone say, "That fellow is the king of the Moriscos. It's no wonder he was living so piously up on a mountain!"

There were other such stupid remarks. We arrived at a place where everybody had come out to have a good look at me. Some were sorry for me, but others jeered.

They put me in the prison for the night under a strong guard, and I spent the night examining my conscience and recommending my life to God.

Why had I been seized, and with such great precautions? And why the royal warrant? I could not make out what it was all about, though I made a hundred guesses.

† I AM A PRISONER IN MADRID †

The next day, I asked for my friend the sheriff to visit me. I wanted him to tell me if he knew why I had been put in prison. He told me that it was, so he thought, something to do with the Moriscos.

Suddenly, I remembered Hornachos, and I concluded that it must be about the arms I had found there. I said to him, "If it is about the arms I found at Hornachos, why on earth have they arrested me with such tactics and with such great numbers? If they had asked me about it at the time, I would gladly have told them everything I knew."

This astonished the sheriff, and he sent for Llerena and repeated to him what I had just said. Llerene jumped for joy and ordered that the arm and leg irons be taken off straightaway. Those irons were an invention of the devil.

They put a prison meal in front of me, but as I was only used to herbs when I ate it my stomach swelled so much that they thought that I was poisoned and was going to die. They sent for a doctor, who carefully examined me and found out what was wrong. He explained that I should eat light food for some time. We went off to Madrid, and I was treated well enough on the road, but I had to wear the irons and had twelve musketeers to guard me.

When we got to Madrid, I walked to the house of the magistrate, Madera, who had just returned from Hornachos. His house was on the Street of the Fountains. When I got there, he had my irons taken off and led me into a room where we could be alone together. He asked me amiably why I had become a hermit. I told him, just as I have explained to you. Then he went on and asked me if I had ever been at Hornachos. I replied, "Sir, if you are really asking me about the arms I found in a corn cellar while passing through there some five years ago with my company, don't worry your head about it. I'll tell you everything that happened."

He stood up and threw his arms around my neck, saying that I was more an angel than a man and that God must have preserved me to lay bare the wickedness and conspiracies of the Moriscos. I then set about telling him everything concerning the affair. Afterward, he had me taken to the house of another court police official, a Señor Alonso Ronquillo; this time I had a guard of six men but no irons.

Orders were given for me to be looked after well and for a doctor to be present at my lunch and dinner. This doctor was very strict. I could not eat or drink what I liked, but only the things that he liked. By what finally reached my stomach, I concluded that a poor man gets a better meal than a rich one.

Four days passed, and I was not allowed to write or even send a message to any of my friends, not even to my mother. Then the same magistrate visited me with a secretary of the criminal court, a Juan de Pina. He put me through a detailed questioning and prepared a statement for me to sign. He would not allow me to use my name of Brother Alonso of the Mother of God, but insisted on that of Alonso de Contreras, sergeant major of Sardinia.

A fortnight later, I was able to write to my mother and to my friends. And, although I was still under surveillance, at least I no longer had a doctor to dine with me.

At midnight one night, Ronquillo came into my room. He was dressed in traveling clothes and with pistols at his hips. With him were six men, similarly fitted out.

"Señor sergeant major," he said, "please get dressed; we have business to do."

When I saw all this traveling gear, I remarked, "But, Señor, what is happening?"

"Dress yourself," he repeated, "we have things to do."

Dressing was, for me, no great trial. I had only to throw a habit over my shoulders, and, when that was done, I said, "Your grace, please tell me where we are going."

"We are going," he replied, "where the court has ordered us to go."

"Would your grace send me to San Ginés then," I asked, "to find a priest to confess to? I shall not leave without at least that."

He turned to me and said, "Come along, it's late, and you'll have no need of confession tonight."

Even with that, I still feared that he was going to take me out of the town and string me up.

CHAPTER TEN

However, in the end, they took me along to San Ginés, which was only three doors away, and the vicar heard my confession. I wish to God that I were today, while I am writing this, even one-quarter as well-prepared to face the Judgment as I was in those days.

I begged and pleaded with my confessor to let me go the next day to find both Secretary Prada and my mother and tell them all that I had told him. I also wanted them to go on defending my name and prevent the words "traitor to the king" ever being linked to it. After that, the vicar went his way and I had another leg iron clapped on.

I was taken back to the house where I had been kept. Before setting off, I was put on a mule and strapped tightly down with my free leg bound under its belly. We crossed the Mayor Square and then went down the Toledo Road, past the Puerto Cerrada, and then up the road where all men condemned to be hanged went. It was, for this reason, called calle de los Ajusticiados. Admittedly, it was also the road which led to the Segovia Gate, and to Hornachos. It was to Hornachos that I was being taken, but I did not then know it. The police officer could have told me and spared all my fears of hanging. We followed this road for all that remained of that night. Each silhouette of a tree I thought was a gibbet.

At dawn we were at Móstoles, but we did not stop there. We went on as far as Casarubios before breakfasting and feeding our mules. I, for one, had no appetite.

I again asked the police officer why he would not tell me where we were going and if he could release me from the agony in which I had spent the night.

"We are going," he said, "to a place, the name of which I cannot tell you till we get there. Those are my orders from the council."

And so I was left in suspense.

We continued our journey until we came in sight of Hornachos, and then the officer said to me, "That's where you're going. And tonight the law goes into action. We shall not go into the town until midnight."

That gave me plenty more to think about while we were waiting, hidden in a garden, for that hour which I believed to be my last. But I was not perturbed. When my time comes, may it please God to find me as well prepared and I shall die content.

At the outskirts of the village, the police officer freed me of my irons and cords and said to me, "Would you please show us the house where you found the muskets?"

"Señor," I replied, "I do not know the village. I only spent one afternoon and one night there and when the soldier took me to this house it was dark and in any case it all happened five years ago. But still, put me on the upper road by the fountain and I will try, with the help of God, to find it."

He took me there, and I said, pointing out two houses, "It is either this one, or that one."

"Good," he said. "Now let us go to the inn."

He gave me dinner, but, curse him, I could only eat a little under the circumstances.

The next day, the police officer worked out a scheme where I could go into the two houses I had pointed out to him. I had to find out which was the one with the arms cellar. This is how it was done.

I first had to go into several other homes and say that I was sent by the bishop of Badajoz to visit the houses to see whether they were well supplied with crucifixes and religious pictures. Since I was dressed in a hermit's habit, they believed me. When news of what I was doing got around, Hornachos was flooded with peddlers, who grew rich overnight selling religious prints. There was not a door left in Hornachos without two or three crucifixes on it. So many were there that it reminded me of a cemetery on some bloody battleground.

Eventually, I went into the right house and discovered the corn cellar. But it was quite different from the way I had described it in my statements. It used to be as white as a dove and about thirty feet long by twenty feet wide.

I was completely at a loss. I leaned against the wall and started scratching it like some prisoner under a life sentence. Then, by the grace of God, a piece of mud fell down and underneath it was quite white. When I saw this, I scraped the mud off the other walls and found three white and one black. I said to Ronquillo, "Señor, please have a man sent down here to knock down this mud wall."

This was done, and the corn cellar was just as I had described it. But it had been cut in half by a wall, and the walls of the first room had been covered with mud.

The owner of the house was arrested. He said that he had bought the house two years before from another Morisco, whose name I do not remember. We wanted to arrest that man, too, but when he heard that part of the house had been pulled down he got on his mare and fled to Portugal. It was only at great cost that he was eventually brought back. Meanwhile, his goods were sequestered and the police officer and guards helped themselves.

After all that, I was no longer kept under strict guard and the police officer, being delighted with the outcome, sent off news of all the things I have described to you to the court.

† I AM PUT ON THE RACK †

As for myself, I was ill; in fact, on the verge of death. But I was looked after with so much care and filled with so many medicines that I became stronger. I was then called for by the court, but, as I was still convalescing, a doctor was sent to look after me on the journey. At every stopping place on the road to Madrid, a sheriff or magistrate came out to meet me and entertained me until it was time to leave. I was honored and slept in the houses of the rich, and I never once set foot inside a jail for the whole journey.

We got to Madrid, and I was led to the same house I had been in before. My mother came to see me and burst into floods of tears. I was, however, by then feeling much better and was taken to the president of Castille's house. He was a man by the name of Don Pedro Manso and, at his house, both the Royal Council and the Council of War were awaiting me. Don Diego de Ibarra and the count of Salazar were sitting in the Council of War, but I did not know any of the others except the treasurer, Don Melchor de Molina.

The commissariat captain to whom I had reported the arms find in Hornachos was brought into the court, and he denied that he had ever been to Hornachos. My statement was then read aloud, and I was asked if I still wished to stand by it. To that I replied, "I know the captain very well and what is more, everything in my statement is quite true. Why," I added, "does he deny a thing which is so obviously true?"

But he denied it fast enough. I replied, "Sir, what I have said is true. But if I must suffer before you find out the truth for yourselves, I am quite prepared."

With that, the court was adjourned, and I was taken back to my usual prison and the commissariat captain to the court jail.

A night or two later, when I had gone to bed, there was a knock at my door and I was told to get dressed. I was carried in a litter to the Street of the Fountains (where I had been before) and found myself in a room beautifully furnished with heavy hangings. There I saw a table on which there was a crucifix, with a candle on each side of it, and an ink pot, powder, and paper.

I then looked up and saw a rack. Next to the rack, I saw the magistrate with his clerk and an executioner. The magistrate exhorted me to tell the truth and, even though it would grieve his soul, he told me he would have to torture me. He told me that the commissariat captain still denied that I had told him about the arms. Because of this, they decided to ask me again. The magistrate then gave the order to go ahead. The clerk read out some formal statement, which I do not remember, and the executioner stripped me naked. He then laid me down on the rack and fixed the cords onto my arms and legs.

They started to put me in that measure of discomfort which would encourage me to say whom I had told about the arms. I still said, "Everything is true in my statement."

The magistrate replied, "I know that you and your captain were given four thousand ducats to keep your mouths shut."

"Nonsense," I said. "My captain knew no more about the affair than the Grand Turk himself. I've told you the truth once." After that, I did not say another word all the time except, "It's a fine thing to torture a man for telling the truth. I needn't have told you any of this in the first place. If you want me to unsay it, I unsay it."

"Tighter, and give it another turn," was the magistrate's only reply.

But this second turn did not seem to hurt me much. Then he gave the order to release me. As I was put in my litter, the magistrate embraced me, and I was taken back to my house, where I was looked after and entertained like a king.

† I FLEE MADRID †

I treated myself very delicately for more than ten days in bed, and then I got up. All this while, the commissariat captain was languishing in the court jail, but on his side he had the old duke of Frias, Condestable of Castille, the count of the Rhine, and an old man. He also had the thirty thousand ducats that he was said to possess.

I was soon released on the understanding that I would not leave Madrid without permission. I was not allowed to wear my hermit's habit anymore but was given in its stead an excellent velvet suit cut in the military style. I was also given four gold *escudos* a day for my board and lodging, which Secretary Pina paid me regularly every fourth day. This allowance was paid out of the property sequestered from the Moriscos.

I went out to the church of San Felipe, dressed as I have already described, and everyone was openmouthed with astonishment at seeing me. They cheered when they realized I was free.

I had to report every evening to the police officer who had been my jailer. One evening, his wife said to me, "Señor, the commissariat captain is gathering dozens of witnesses to prove that he has never been to Hornachos and, as you have eaten at our table, I advise you as a good friend to escape while you can and not risk prison again. And as the old saying goes, 'It is better to hide in the woods than to trust the prayers of good men.'"

Well, I believed she was doing her best for me and, by God, I wasted no time following her advice. But it turned out that the commissariat captain had bribed her, for he was a rich man as I have told you, and, in this way, she completed his campaign against me.

I had saved a little money and I begged two days' pay off Secretary Pina, saying that I was very hard up. I then sold my black velvet suit and bought in the calle de las Postas a letter carrier's suit, cloak, leggings, and a poor man's sword.

That night, at sundown, with a mailbag on my back and a rough cap on my head, I left Madrid and struck out for Alicante. It was January and anyone who has walked that road in the winter will feel sorry for me.

† I PROVE MY INNOCENCE †

At dawn, I crossed by the Bayona ferry and went on through La Mancha. At Albicete, I turned off toward Alicante. In all, the journey took four days.

I already knew that the regiments of Italy plus the Armada regiment were stationed near Valencia, so I set about finding out exactly where they were. I knew that many men from my Hornachos company had transferred to the Armada regiment at Lisbon, when the company was disbanded.

I learned that the regiment was in the Cortes Mountains. So off I went, as I have already told you, dressed as a letter carrier. Every day, I searched every face in the companies as they went on guard duty and among them I found fifteen of my old comrades, of which two were lieutenants on the active list.

I told my woes to these lieutenants, and they sympathized with me and took me to their inn. I then went on to tell them that the commissariat captain was saying he had never been to Hornachos.

"He's lying," they said. "We can remember the inn he had his breakfast in and even what he ate that morning."

I spoke with several of the soldiers and they said what they had to say about it, and I prepared an affidavit for the regimental attorney to verify and seal. I explained to him that it was a matter of my coming into some property and I had to prove that the captain had been in Hornachos at a certain time. I put my request to the attorney in the proper manner and put the witnesses at his disposal. The outcome of it was that I got a statement sworn by five witnesses that the captain had been in Hornachos at the same time as my company. I then packed it away in my bag and thought about returning to Madrid. But I decided to stay on for two reasons. One, it was rumored that the Moriscos who were living in the mountains were going to lose their civil rights and that at any moment we were going to pillage their lands. And, two, the weather was bitterly cold.

My disappearance from Madrid was noticed after two days. The authorities searched everywhere for me and finally had my name shouted all over Madrid by the town crier. Because I did not reply and no one knew where I was (they had found a few clues which made them think I had gone towards Valencia), the commissariat captain asked to be released, saying, "Contreras told a pack of lies, and now he's off to join the Morisco rebellions."

The rascal, having plenty of money and two great lords to support his cause, was released without difficulty. All the same, the magistrate did not believe that I had gone to join the Moriscos and had a secret inquiry made into my ancestry. He traced me back as far as four generations to see if there was any Jewish or Moorish blood in my veins.

I tell you this because, some time later, Secretary Pina said to me, "If you had the money it cost us to research and inquire into your birth, your parents' birth, and your paternal and maternal ancestors, you could live like a lord for quite a while. Anyhow, it was lucky for you that we found nothing suspicious in your lineage, because if we had you would have been hanged without a doubt."

All the same, the captain was let out of jail and everyone condemned the Moriscos, saying that they ought to be thrown out of Spain. But as for me, they still carried on their search.

A few days later, during a little raid on the Moriscos, a high-spirited stallion mule fell into my hands. I broke it in and rode off to Albacete, but first I got a letter from the sergeant major of the regiment stating that I was not on active duty in that regiment and that the mule I was riding, of such and such description, was looted from the Moriscos. Without question, it was mine to own or dispose of. At Albacete, I sold it for thirty-six ducats, though it was worth a good hundred.

I next went on foot to Madrid. At Vallecas, three miles from Madrid, I wrote a petition and addressed it to the king, by courtesy of Secretary Don Andrés Prada.

That night at dusk, with my bag on my back, I entered Madrid. I went straight to the house of the count of Salazar and asked to see his secretary. When he recognized me, he said, "For God's sake, clear out of the town. If you are caught you will be hanged tomorrow!"

I said, "No," but he would not listen to any of my arguments. He just kept telling me to get out of town. So I soon gave up and called a page boy, instructing him to tell the count that a courier had arrived from the army in Valencia.

The count had me come in immediately. When he recognized me, he became apprehensive and looked from one side of the room to the other as though he were hoping to find some help if it were needed.

"Señor," I said to him, "I am Lieutenant Contreras, and I have come like this (I had mud up to my knees) to defend my reputation and to put before your lordship some new evidence. I can prove that the commissariat captain was at Hornachos at the time I said he was. I left Madrid without authority only so that I could find some soldiers of my company who could bear witness in my favor. I now remain at your lordship's disposal."

"By my order of knighthood," he said, "I have always held a good opinion of you, Contreras. Now go to Melchor de Molina, the treasurer, and tell him all you've told me and see me again tomorrow."

I went to de Molina's house, but I was told that he was asleep, so I went off to see a woman I knew. I knocked at her door and a maidservant was sent to open it. When she saw me, she was terrified and shrieked, "Oh, my God, it's the lieutenant!"

Filthy as I was, and scarcely recognizable, I was let into the house, where the woman I had come to see nearly became hysterical.

"What is all the fuss about?" I asked.

"You are mad to come to Madrid," the woman said. "They will catch you and hang you and that is one good reason for the fuss. God's grief, go to a church and take asylum there!"

"Now, now, Isabelilla," I said calmly, "you send along to the English ambassador's kitchen and get me a meat paté and some wine as I am dying of hunger. If I am going to be hanged, I might as well die with a full belly."

She sent her maidservant, who came back in the twinkling of an eye with the paté and the wine.

"Now sit down and have some dinner, Isabelilla," I said.

She said she had already eaten, so I set about my meal. Afterward, I washed my feet in a little wine and went to bed. I was very tired and slept well. I was up early the next morning, but not as early as the treasurer, who had already left his house when I got there. I was told that he had gone to mass at the Jesuit church. I went there and waited until he came out, and then went up to him and explained that I had a sworn statement. The count had told me to give it to him and that he and the count would be meeting that morning at the palace.

He took the statement and told me how sorry he was to see me in such a plight. He then told me to wait for him in his house. I did as he ordered.

The servant of the woman with whom I had eaten the night before was a good friend of the bailiff. She had warned him first thing in the morning that I was back and that I was going to see the treasurer.

The bailiff warned his master who was a court police officer called Artiaga, and the two of them plus other bailiffs gathered to catch me as I left the treasurer's house. I waited for the treasurer until nearly noon. As soon as he had got down from his carriage, he saw me and said, "Come with me, his majesty wants to do you an honor."

As he said this, he grasped my hand, and those who were with him were astonished to see him do such a thing to a man who looked like an unhorsed letter carrier—or worse. We went inside to his study and sat down. He said many flattering things about my courage and then remarked, "Please go now and see the count; we have all put our heads together at the palace and we have come to a decision concerning you which the count will inform you of."

As I was leaving the house, the police officer and the bailiffs attacked me, shouting, "In the name of the king, surrender!"

I gripped the hilt of my sword, drew it and kept them all at bay. I thought that the treasurer had laid a trap for me, so I let no one come near me at all. Then the treasurer was informed of what was happening in front of his house and he came out, shouting, "You rogues and ruffians, what are you doing? Don't you know who this man is dressed as a courier? Isn't it enough for you that he comes as a free man out of my house? If I have any more of this insult, I'll have you all thrown into the galleys!"

The police officer stood there stupefied by what had happened. I put away my cheap sword and went off to the count's house with more than a hundred people, some in front of me leading the way, and others following in procession. All this crowd waited with me until the count arrived and then they went their way.

"Come up to my study, lieutenant," the count said. Next, we went upstairs and he said, "You have behaved yourself as a man of great honor. Everything has been thought over now: just tell us where you would like to have a company of infantry and you will be given the title of captain."

I kissed his hand for the honor, and said, "Señor, if this is the way things are to be, I choose Flanders."

He gave me a letter for Secretary Prada, and three hundred *reales* in pieces of two as well. I went straight away to see the secretary and gave him the letter. He gave me another letter addressed to the king, who was then at the Prado.

I went to the Prado and handed my letter to the king's secretary, who told me to come back to his office at nightfall. I went there as I was told, and he gave me a letter for Secretary Prada and a thousand *reales* in pieces of four. I took both the letter and the money with me back to Madrid and delivered the letter to Prada. Enclosed in the letter was my captaincy for Flanders, with an increase of twelve *escudos* in my pay and a letter to the archduke from the king ordering him to give me a company of infantry.

I dressed myself as a soldier again and again asked my mother to give me her blessing. I left her some of the money I had been given and took the road for Agreda, where I had been a hermit.

As for the commissariat captain, he had both money and good guardian angels. Laws had by then been passed to banish the Moriscos from Spain, so the charge against him became less serious. He was at that time on parole but was eventually banished from the court; however, he could not have been banished for long, as I met the rogue in Madrid scarcely more than four years later.

CHAPTER ELEVEN

I left Madrid and took the road to Agreda. In a very few days, I arrived. When the people of the town knew that I was staying at a local inn, and much more importantly when they heard that I had been honored by the king and given a new commission, they were all delighted to see me.

I stayed with them five days and then went on to the port of San Sebastian. I embarked there on a ship from Dunkirk and reached Flanders in a week. I went on to Brussels and presented my letters to the archduke. He welcomed me very generously and agreed to put me on his payroll. I had his promise that I should have a company as soon as possible. While I was waiting for a company, I enrolled as a lieutenant in Captain Andrés de Prada's company. (He was a relative of the secretary of state.) The regiment, whose colonel was Don Juan de Menéses, was at the time on garrison duty at Cambrai.

For two whole years, I stayed there, and not once did we go campaigning. I did not get my company either. We had to await the outcome of King Henry IV of France's passion for the duchess of Condé; only he knew whether he would marry her and there would be no war. Neither did we know what his new policy would be.

The duchess of Condé at that time had already fled for safety to the infanta's court at Brussels, along with her husband the duke of Condé. The duke should have inherited the crown of France, had not Henry IV taken it from him.

Here is an opportunity to tell a tale about Henry IV. It was a remarkable thing, and I swore to the truth of the story at the time to the magistrates at Cambrai.

Henry had come to Paris with many of his Navarre countrymen and was married to Margaret de Valois. Seven days later, the Queen Mother, Catherine déMedici, began the St. Bartholomew's Day massacre, in which Henry's followers in Paris and thousands of Protestants throughout France were slaughtered.

After that, France fell into the hands of the Duc de Guise, and the Catholic League. However, the king, Henry III, succeeded in regaining much of his power, but he never forgave the league. Just before his own assassination, the effete Henry III had the Duc de Guise and the Cardinal of Lorraine assassinated. It was an act that his mother on her deathbed deplored, because she saw that it meant that power in France would swing in the favor of the Huguenots. Before Henry III died, he recognized Henry of Navarre as his successor and recommended him to become a Catholic.

The French were not happy about this Henry, but after the calamities of the past they would have accepted any king who was not an idiot, and who was wholly masculine. Henry of Navarre was ambitious and not a man of fixed opinions. He did become a Catholic. He divorced his first wife, Margaret de Valois, on the grounds that she had provided him no heir. In 1600, he married Maria déMedici (by whom he had a son who was to become Louis XIII), and so produced a new Catholic Bourbon dynasty.

During this Henry's reign, the industrial and fiscal program of Sully put France back on its feet and put gold at the disposal of the king. All revolts were crushed, and, as soon as Sully had enough in the treasury,

Henry started his attacks on the Hapsburgs. However, as Contreras tells
us, this was brought to an abrupt end.

As you know, in 1610 Henry had made a pact with Germany
and Italy against the Hapsburgs and in particular with an eye to
taking Flanders. His ex-queen, Margaret de Valois, was not then
in favor, and Henry went one day to St. Denis, where he kept her,
to get an oath of allegiance. On that day, he returned to Paris; it
was only a distance of six miles. But once in the city, going down a
narrow street, where his carriage could not properly be protected
by his bodyguard, a man rushed out and attacked him with a
butcher's knife. The king cried, "Don't kill me," and straightaway
the assassin made a second thrust. So died the bravest king there
had been for two hundred years.

The man was captured and slowly tortured until he died.
Every day they gave him some new and hellish treatment, but the
most he ever said in answer to the agony was, "My God of
Paradise."

Whenever he was asked who had urged him to kill the king, he
replied, "No one. I did it so that Christians should not suffer.
Twice before I have come from my native town to do this, but I
had no opportunity; on both occasions I spent all I had and
returned home."

This man was called François Ravaillac, a native of Angoûleme
in Brittany; he was a schoolmaster. The murder took place at four
o'clock in the afternoon on 14 May 1610. I was then at Cambrai,
which was quite near, and I confirmed it.

Now I will tell you about the remarkable thing that I saw while
on garrison duty with my regiment at Cambrai.

We had just received orders to get ready to go on campaign—a
thing we had prayed for as often as we had prayed for a place in
heaven. That night when our company was on guard duty, I and
another lieutenant, Juan Jul by name, a Majorcan, went to inspect
the guards on the city wall. We went up on the ramparts, where

there were several sentry posts, and when we got to the Péronne Gate we heard the sound of a courier's bugle. We were very pleased, as we hoped it might be our marching orders.

When the courier hailed us, we asked, "Where do you come from?"

"From Spain," was his answer.

It was possible. He had come on the right road. Then we asked him, "Have you any letters for the governor?"

"No," he replied, "And don't stop me now."

"Well," we asked, "what is the news?"

"Tonight," he replied, "the king of France was twice stabbed and died."

The other lieutenant and I agreed that I, being the faster runner, should go and tell the governor. When I got to his house he was in bed, but I told him the news. He was very perturbed, as he knew what a dangerous political situation we were in.

After talking with the governor, I went back to the ramparts. Meeting up with the lieutenant, we continued on our rounds and passed on the news to all the guardrooms. Everyone was amazed at our story.

By the next day, word had gotten around, and the peasants came to Cambrai bringing all their possessions on carts to put them somewhere safe. They said, "Now the king is dead. There is nothing to hold his soldiery in check and they will come and loot our homes."

But for all that, the report of the king's death turned out not to be true. And everyone laughed at my expense.

Then, nine days after that happened, a servant of Don Inigo de Cardenas, the Spanish ambassador in Paris, brought some news. He told us the earlier version of the king's death, without variation on a single point. He added that the ambassador's house had been put under the guard of two companies, just in case the people of Paris should take it into their heads that the ambassador had instigated the murder and kill him and all his household.

The coincidence was astounding.

† I AM NEARLY HANGED †

We then went out campaigning until September. I asked the archduke to let me go to Malta, where I had heard that a chapter general was being held and where I hoped to gather the fruits of the work I had done for the Religion.

I got permission to leave, but because I had no money to buy horses, whether I went alone or with a servant, I decided to go as a pilgrim. I therefore dressed myself as a French pilgrim, because I spoke French well, hid a sword in the center of my staff, put my papers in a haversack, and set off.

I reached a town called Creil, which was between Amiens and Paris. The duke of Condé and his wife had gone back there now that there was no longer any danger from Henry IV. I asked the duke if he would be so kind as to give me a letter of recommendation to the grand master at Malta. He gave me one, and it was no longer nor broader than a finger. He also gave me three hundred *reales*. I soon went through Burgundy and reached Châlons. When I reached the town gate, it was closed, so I walked along the banks of the river which flowed beneath the city walls, looking for another entrance.

As I walked, my curiosity was aroused, and I got deeply absorbed studying the city's fortifications. I was observed, and when I reached the next gate I was arrested. Here I had done nothing wrong at all. When they wanted to take my staff, I resisted them and they shouted, "This *bougre* is a Spanish spy!"

We battled over the staff so much that it came apart and they saw the sword. Then, they were sure beyond any question that I was a spy.

They dragged me off to the prison, and some thought they ought to put me on the rack. Others thought I should hang. Was any other proof needed, they said. I had been caught with a concealed sword.

I showed them my papers and my ticket of leave from the archduke, but that made no difference. Finally, a Spaniard took pity on me. This man had married and settled down in Châlons; in point of fact, he could not go back to Spanish lands as he had mutinied in Flanders and been declared a traitor. He came to me and said, "You must keep your wits about you, sir; these people want to hang you. Is there anything you would like me to do for you?"

I could not believe that he was not joking. But when I realized that both he and my captors were deadly serious, I almost went mad at the thought of so meaningless a death.

"Señor," I told him, "I have a letter of recommendation which the duke of Condé wrote for me to give to the grand master of Malta. As you can see, I am just a traveler and no spy."

"Give it to me," he said.

God's body! It was so small I could hardly find it! However, when I did locate it, he took it off to the magistrates. I waited there as disconsolate as you may well imagine. An hour later, I heard a crowd of people in the prison square, and I felt sure that they were coming to feast their cruel spirits and torture me. I was even more sure when I heard a voice say, "Where is the Spaniard? Bring him here."

I went and there I found all the judges of the town. They said to me in French, "Come with us."

They took me off to an inn, and ordered the innkeeper, who was no more a heretic than Calvin, to wine, dine, and lodge me well. And so he did.

This part of France—Châlons and Lyons—was largely Protestant. That explains Contreras's dry remark about the innkeeper being no more a heretic than Calvin; it also explains why Contreras's letter was respected. Despite the fact that the duke of Condé was an exile in Brussels during Henry IV's time, he was a cousin of the king and a letter from him carried weight as a letter from a member of the ruling family of the kingdom; a family that, though Catholic, had Protestant roots and had legitimized the Protestant faith.

The next day, they sent a horse for myself and two cavalrymen to accompany me as far as Lyons. Everything went excellently, so well in fact that, as far as Lyons, my journey with good food all the way did not cost me a penny. At Lyons, I was handed over to the governor and he did the same for me. He paid my expenses at the inn and two more cavalrymen went as far as the borders of Savoy with me. That is to say, as far as Chambéry.

From there, I carried on to Genoa, where I picked up a boat bound for Naples. I found another ship to take me on to Palermo, where the duke of Ossuna was viceroy. I called to see him and pay my respects, and when he saw my papers he made me a present of a hundred ducats.

But despite that sign of favor, there were some who wanted to see the back of me. They told me that the viceroy had given orders to have me arrested on the charge of my old murders. It turned out not to have been true, but I did not wait to find out and I got aboard a ship bound for Malta where I was more welcome.

† I JOIN THE ORDER OF ST. JOHN †

Immediately, I was sent on a scouting expedition; our fleet at the time was on its way to the Kerkennah Isles, which lay off Barbary. I made the trip and reported on everything I had seen and heard.

In 1611, a chapter general was held and I was received into the priory of Castille as a brother servant-at-arms. I was known so well in Malta that I was not asked to furnish any documents of service or of my birth. There was not one vote cast against me out of the whole chapter of more than two hundred knights.

I did my year's novitiate and at the end of it, they gave me the habit of the Order of St. John. Two knights then spoke against me, saying that I had committed two public homicides, but they were overruled by the grand master, and I took my vows.

During that year, I only had one quarrel; it was with a bragging Italian knight. It was all because I took the part of another knight who had done me a good turn. Anyhow, this Italian shot at me twice and missed.

I asked, consequently, for permission to go to Spain, and it was granted. I went as far as Carthagena in one of the galleys of the Religion in the company of the knight whose side I had taken in the quarrel I told you about. He paid my expenses all the way. This knight came with me as far as Madrid, but there would not be enough paper in the whole of Genoa to tell you all the adventures that happened to us on the way.

At Madrid, the knight left me. I entered the city in my new habit of the order, and everyone congratulated me—some out of fondness for me, and others enviously.

I asked the Council of War for an infantry company, but they sent me to serve with the royal fleet. I stayed with the fleet a while, taking a lively part in all that happened, and then returned to Madrid.

† I INSULT A COURT OF LAW †

About this time, I picked myself a married woman as a lover. All went well for several days, until another married woman I knew started slanderous gossip against me out of jealousy. That made me do a disgusting thing: I admit it as such, although I performed it.

I went to the house of the woman who was spreading rumors about me, fully intending to slash her face in front of her husband. I drew my dagger to do so and, when she realized what I was going to do, she buried her head in her skirts between her knees. In annoyance that she had foiled me, I became angry and tossed her skirts over her head. Her being bent down lent itself admirably to my deed, and I took two slashes at her bottom as though I were cutting a melon.

Her husband found his sword and made after me. But he did not succeed in catching me, so he went to the sergeant at arms and laid a charge against me. There were always plenty of them with no work to do and they went out to find me. I took up a strong defensive position at the door of a house, and let no one pass through unless he was willing to let my sword pass through him first. The longer I held firm, the greater the crowd of city police and court police became, until finally one of the court magistrates, Don Farinas, was called. He approached me with a crowd of police to support him and, with his hat in hand, said to me politely, "I beg your grace to put your sword back in its scabbard."

To which I replied, "Your grace is so courteous that if I lose my head for doing so, I will put my sword away."

I did so and he said, "Swear to me on this cross that you will not escape and that you will come with me."

"A man," I replied, "who has done just as he is asked has no need to swear promises. I will go wherever you please."

Off we went side by side to the court prison and when we got there he said, "Your grace may stay here until I have spoken with his highness the prince, grand prior of Castille. . . . Hey there!" Don Farinas called to the prison servants, "Give this gentleman a room, the best one you have." And to me he said, "God be with you, and I shall see you again this evening."

The warder then came to me and said, "If your grace would like some company, there are some Genoese knights here."

I said I would, and we went up to their rooms. I asked them if I might join them, and they said they would be delighted.

I sent a note to the secretary of the priory of Castille, telling him of what had happened, but he already knew. The Genoese knights gave me a good dinner and let me make up a bed on the floor, which was not as bad as it might have been.

At midnight a magistrate on his way to torture a robber called and started asking me questions.

"Your grace knows quite well," I told him, "that the day I put on the habit of the Order of St. John and took my vows I gave up my legal freedom and that I can only be tried by a court of the Religion. Therefore, I pray you take me to the prince, our grand prior, who is my rightful judge."

"If you go on talking like that," he said, "heaven knows what will happen to you."

"What I have said," I replied, "I stand by and I'll sign my name to it if you want me to."

And that was the end of the questioning. The magistrate went home, and I went back to bed. The next morning the same magistrate came to me in a great flurry, telling me to get dressed quickly as the tribunal was waiting.

"I am *not* going," I replied, "because those gentlemen are *not* my judges."

He went off to report my words to the tribunal, and they sent him back with eight galley slaves to carry me and my bedding bodily into the court. This I could not stop them from doing.

I was put down in the middle of the courtroom, still in bed just as I had been in the prison. They then started to say to me all the usual things that courts say, but I replied only one word. It was a word, such as I will not write down here, but it was of sufficient contempt for them to have me carried off immediately to be put in a dungeon.

As I was going down a passage way, I met two knights of my order and the treasurer, who were on their way to reclaim my body by order of the priory of Castille.

We all went into the courtroom, and behind locked doors they petitioned for my being handed over to them. A magistrate was sent to the Council of War to report on the situation. One of the knights, called de Valenzuela, went at the same time to the king.

We waited all morning, the court having discontinued its inquiry, but at noon de Valenzuela came back bringing a royal decree. I have, by the way, still got a copy of it. It read:

"Hand over Lieutenant Alonso de Contreras to the prince, the grand prior, my nephew, with all his written statements, provided that the court is satisfied that he has taken his vows in the Religion. If this be so, a copy of the certificate stating so, should be retained by the court."

So I had again to appear before the judge—this time fully dressed—and I was asked for my certificate of acceptance into the Religion. I had it sent for and, after the court all had a look at it and agreed that it was valid, they put me in the hands of the knights, who led me off to the royal jail.

There I stayed until the priory called me and condemned me to two years' banishment. I then went to serve in the fleet for the period of my punishment.

† I AM POISONED IN ROME †

After two years, I asked permission to return to the court to ask for a captaincy. Forty captains were nominated, but no luck came my way, so I left Madrid intending to go to Malta where my chances might be better. On my way, I fell in with a knight also on his way to my destination. We joined company and went on to Barcelona, where we found a ship sailing for Genoa. From Genoa, we went by land to Rome, which only took a few days. Then an annoying thing happened: I fell sick with malaria. But as I was by no means bedridden by it, I passed the time at the house of some Spanish ladies I knew.

One day, while I was talking with these Spanish ladies, some Italian gentlemen, unknown to me or the women, were let in by the servant. They came into the room we were in and said to me, "What are you doing here?"

"I am talking about Spain," I said, "with these ladies, who are fellow countryfolk of mine."

"Out you get," one of them said to me brusquely.

To leave on such orders seemed to me rather a shameful thing to do, so I turned a deaf ear and went on talking with the Spanish women.

"Are you waiting for us to throw you downstairs?" they demanded.

By this time, even though I was ill and only able to hold my sword weakly, I could stand no more of their insults. I got up and went for them and knocked them both backward down the stairs. One of them cracked his head. On hearing their yells and moans, one of the many police patrols in Rome came up, arrested us and bundled us, women and all, into a carriage and took us to the governor. The whole story was then explained to him.

No charge was preferred as the women and the men, too, offered to shake hands and forget the whole affair. This we did and returned to our own homes.

But these Italians, lacking the courage to take me on openly, plotted with my innkeeper to have me die another way. They had the innkeeper tell me that there was a doctor who guaranteed to cure me of malaria in four days. And if there was no cure, there would be no payment.

I wanted to get well again quickly, so I said, "Bring him along."

The next day my innkeeper came into my room and remarked, "The doctor has come to see you."

In he came. He was dressed in clerical dress. He examined me and asked me about my illness and I told him everything.

"I'll have you fit in four days," he said as he was leaving, and then, "God be with you. I shall see you again tomorrow, but meantime stay in bed."

He left, and then my host said, "He's the finest doctor in Rome, you know; he's Cardinal de Joyosa's physician."

I waited patiently until the next day for this doctor or devil, whichever you want to call him. He came and took out of his doctor's bag a little vial of red wine and a piece of paper containing a powder. He asked for a glass and poured in lots of the powder. He then poured in the wine and mixed it up giving it to me. Then he said, "Drink it up, my lord."

I swallowed it down and, when I had finished the draft, he remarked, "Keep yourself warm and you are as good as cured." Then he went away.

In less than ten minutes, my teeth began to chatter and my bowels to gripe so much that I feared I was going to die like a dog. I sent for a priest to make my confession. I vomited violently and passed inky excrement.

As soon as my comrade heard of the trouble, he ran to the Spanish embassy and called the ambassador's doctor, a Portuguese. He came straightaway, and I told him what had happened. After he had seen what my stomach had rejected in both directions, he prescribed medicines. And thanks to his prescriptions, my illness went away.

Later, he said to me, to explain how sick I felt, "If I gave a mule as much of that powder as goes into a walnut shell, it would die in an hour."

And I had been given a tablespoonful!

The doctor continued to visit me until I was on my feet again. As he was interested in tracing and arresting this false doctor, he asked my innkeeper what he knew about him.

"I had never seen him before," he replied. "But he came here and offered his services, saying that he was the Cardinal de Joyosa's doctor. What I did, I only did for the best."

However, that doctor was never seen again, and I could only conclude that he had been sent by the two men I had knocked down the stairs.

And so the matter rested. I got stronger and set off for Naples with my comrade, and from there we went to Messina and finally reached Malta.

CHAPTER
TWELVE

There were some letters from Spain waiting for me at Malta. Among them was one from the king to the grand master asking him to give me leave to go back to Spain to raise a company of infantry. I was, after all, one of eight lieutenants to be promoted to the rank of captain.

Another letter was addressed to me from Don Bartholomé de Anaya of the Council of War, and it gave official notification of my appointment. I set about my preparations for travel once again and sailed within a fortnight. The grand master instructed me to go through Marseilles and to tell the two galleys of the Religion, which were there, to sail in complete secrecy to Carthagena to collect 200,000 ducats, which had fallen due to the order, and to bring the money to Malta.

I reached Madrid from Malta in twenty-seven days, by way of Barcelona, but when I got there I found that a cousin of mine, a lieutenant who had served in Flanders, had already gone off to Osuna to raise my company for me. As he had not been given a company of his own, he had offered to raise mine in my name, with the rank of lieutenant, on the understanding that if I did not appear before the embarkation date he was to remain in charge.

Knowing that I was far off, the council had agreed. But I made such good speed that I got there four months before the day we were to have embarked to go to the Philippine Islands.

When I arrived at Osuna with my commission, which had been given me in Madrid, my cousin nearly died when he saw me. After all, he was thinking how near he had been to becoming a captain. We talked, and I offered to do everything I could for him, as should be the case with a relative and a good friend. He told me how he was looking forward to the expedition and I thought well of him. But I did not know the damnable tricks he was up to.

He got to my page, who was also my lance carrier, and inveigled him into giving me arsenic. The first time the boy did it, he poured it on my eggs in this manner. The eggs were soft-boiled and taken out of their shells. The page then powdered them with arsenic and sugar. I crumbled my bread on them as I always did, and ate them. An hour later, I felt so ill that I thought I was going to die. I called the doctor and made my confession to a priest all in an hour, thinking I was going to expire that night. The whole town sent me their sympathy.

At midnight, they gave me a thick fruit cordial, but the little rascal had run off to the chemist and bought some more arsenic and poured a few pennyworth into my drink. I drank some of it, but it burned four sores into my throat and I could not finish it. The doctors did not know what to think. They went to the chemist to ask what he had put in the cordial, to which he replied, "Only what you told me to put in it."

They then made me take a draft to make me vomit, but it was not necessary, as nature had already done that for me and had been the real cure.

The next day, the governor and all the important people of the town came to visit. The governor, unknown to me, had the woman who was doing the cooking in my house arrested and gave orders that my food should come from his own kitchens. But at lunch time, the little page again found my plate of food and put another packet of arsenic in it.

I ate one mouthful and immediately started being sick again. This vomiting was assumed to have been caused by the other meals in which there had been arsenic.

As it was August and very hot, I had a soldier around who fanned me and kept off the flies. The man was called Nieto, and, at that time, he, too, was feeling ill in the nether regions.

"Give it to me," he said. "I'll eat it, meat and all, even though it is Friday."

Well, the poor fellow ate my almost untouched lunch, and at five o'clock that evening he died.

During all the time that I was ill, my cousin did not visit me at all. I handed over all my possessions to the magistrate with verbal instructions of what he was to do in the case of my death, which was just as good as a formal will. Then my page boy went to the magistrate and said to him, "Sir, my master sends me to ask you to give me the key of his chest, so that I can find an indulgenced rosary he has there."

There was, in actual fact, an indulgenced rosary in my baggage. The magistrate gave him the key and the boy helped himself to six hundred *reales*, a 250-carat Maltese cross, as well as stockings, garters, and cummerbunds. After that, he did not show his face all day.

That evening, the magistrate came to see me and asked, "And how do you feel now?"

"Better," I replied.

But I felt better only because I was no longer being dosed with arsenic. Then, he went on to talk about the rosary and to ask what indulgences were attached to it.

"What rosary?" I asked.

"Didn't you send your page to ask me for the key of your chest to get it out for you?"

"No," I replied.

"Well, I gave it to him," said the magistrate.

A search party was then sent out for the boy, and he was caught at the house of a muleteer, with whom he had just made his arrangements to go to Seville. He was brought in front of me, and I demanded the key back, which he produced. The chest was opened, and all the things I have already mentioned were missing.

"Where have you put all these things?" I asked him.

"I have hidden them," he said, and told us where. Some men went with him and everything was found except twenty-six *reales*.

Then I said, "Empty out his pockets."

This was done, and a packet of arsenic was found. Someone opened it, and the innkeeper's wife recognized it as arsenic and said, "Gentlemen, that is the poison that the captain has been given."

I looked at it, too, and saw that the woman was right. It was arsenic. I turned on the boy.

"You traitor!" I said. "What have I done to you that makes you want to poison me?"

"Sir, I found this packet in the street," he replied.

I then turned to the magistrate and said, "Please send for the hangman, and then we'll get the truth out of all this."

But the magistrate replied, "It would be better, I think, to take him to jail and put him through the usual processes and questionings, under torture if necessary, and we will find out soon enough who's at the bottom of this plot."

That seemed to be reasonable enough, so I sent for my lieutenant, whom I had not seen for two days, and ordered him to take the child off to prison under a guard of four soldiers.

He came with his posse of men and took the boy away, but since he was the root of all the corruption, when he reached the San Domingo Church, he advised the boy to take asylum there. The little rascal did not need to be told twice: He ran in and threw himself on the mercy of the monks. That was not all. The lieutenant begged the Dominican monks, saying, "I pray you do not give the boy up, as the captain will hang him the moment you do."

The monks, when they had heard this, sent the boy off to Seville that same night.

From the time that no more arsenic was put in my food, I started getting better. God preserved me for his own purposes and only He knew what they were. Soon, to the delight of the town, I was able to walk again.

When I felt well enough, I went to Seville with six soldiers to find this boy. We made a systematic search of the town, found him quite easily, and brought him back to Osuna.

Everyone there hoped that an example would be made of him. A court was convened, and the boy was charged. He confessed under torture that my cousin the lieutenant had induced him to poison me by promises of money and position. He was judged to be deserving of hanging, but was not old enough. Eventually, he was bound to a prison post and given a hundred lashes and had the forefinger and thumb of each hand cut off because they were the offending digits that had done the sprinkling.

In my dying confession, I had promised to God to forgive whoever it was who had been the cause of my death. The confessor had dragged it from me knowing it was my cousin. So when the governor wanted to arrest him, I refused to make any charge against him and instead sent for him and said, "Begone and ask no reasons. If there is anything you need, ask for it and I will give it you."

He went as white as a ghost and vanished in less than an hour, not being able to believe that I would not go back on my word. I later heard that he had gone to the Indies; he never again showed his face in Spain.

As for myself, for two years I did not have the proper use of my hands and feet. They tingled unremittingly. The poison had also taken all the strength out of my body. The doctor said that the only reason I was not dead was that my stomach had gotten used to poison during my last visit to Rome.

† MY SHIP SINKS IN CÁDIZ HARBOR †

The captain of commissariat came and reviewed the company, and we marched off toward Sanlúcar, where the fleet, which was to sail for the Philippines, was lying ready at anchor. I was detailed to embark on the galleon *La Concepción,* in command of three companies of infantry. We then sailed to Cádiz, which was our starting-off point for the voyage to the Philippines.

At Cádiz, we got orders from the king telling us not to sail to the Philippines but to join the royal fleet instead. We were to sail in company with the silver galleons and all the Spanish galleys to Gibraltar, where the Dutch fleet was expected. Prince Philibert was the general of the force.

At the entrance to Cádiz Harbor, there is a reef, called Diamond Reef, which is not very far under the water. Many ships have wrecked themselves there. I, by the greatest bad luck, hit it and foundered in full view of the whole squadron. Fortunately, no one drowned, as we were picked up by the longboats of the fleet and by the flagship, which was under the command of the marquis of Santa Cruz.

Prince Philibert gave orders for my arrest, and I was taken aboard his galleon, where I stayed for the whole period of the expedition. And I was not let ashore until the Council of War was satisfied that the sinking was not my fault, and my name was cleared.

We sailed up and down the straits from Gibraltar to Cape Spartel for three months with several other ships of the fleet, waiting for a Dutch fleet that never came.

This cruise started in January 1616, and, in March or April of that year, orders came for the fleet to be split up. In particular, the ships which were to have gone to the Philippines were to sail straightaway, as they were badly needed there.

Six galleons were attached to the royal fleet, and the infantry, which was the best in the world, was ordered to Lombardy under the high command of Don Carlos de Ibarra. The colonel of these 2,500 men was Don Pedro Estaban of Avila.

As for myself, I stayed in Spain with another captain, as the king had sent orders to the marquis of Santa Cruz that read like this: "It is desirable that we should reinforce the regiments in Lombardy. Don Pedro Estaban de Avila should take with him as well as his own troops the companies of Captains Contreras and Cornejo. These captains, being expert navigators, are to remain in Spain to raise more men for the Philippines."

So we did not go to Italy but went under the orders of the marquis to the court. They kept us there six months and at last I was given orders to go to Seville at a moment's notice and to report to the Junta of War for the Indies. I was told that further orders would be sent me while I was on my way. Don Fernando Carillo, president of the *junta,* sent for me and gave me five hundred *escudos* for my journey, and that evening I set off on muleback for Seville.

† TAMING ANDALUSIAN CUTTHROATS †

At Cordova, a courier brought me a letter ordering me to report for further orders to the duke of Medina at Sanlúcar. I saw his excellency, and he ordered me to go in complete secrecy to Cádiz with orders for the governor of Cádiz, adding privately that the infantry at Cádiz was to be embarked on the two galleons. They were to be put aboard at nine o'clock the next day.

I saw the governor. The letter I brought instructed him to spend some money and revictual and equip the companies there. We had the companies assembled, and I had to pick two hundred men; I was to be in command of this new company and of the two galleys. I had no superior officer, not a captain, lieutenant or even a sergeant.

Everything was done in utmost secrecy, and we got the men aboard. Had these ruffians—and they were the dregs of Andalusia—gotten any idea of what was happening, we should not have gotten one of them near a ship.

We marched to Sanlúcar, and the duke had the two galleons ready as he had promised. They were both of four hundred tons and equipped with artillery and food, as well as extra war stores of gunpowder, fuses, and lead, which we were taking to reequip the place we were going to. As soon as I reached Sanlúcar, I was ordered to embark my infantry. This I did, putting one hundred men in each galley so quickly that they scarcely realized what had happened.

The captain of the other galleon then arrived from the court and we, too, embarked for our expedition to the Indies. Our orders were to give help to Puerto Rico, which was being besieged by the Dutch.

I was instructed to wait for my final sailing orders at Los Pozuelos, which was near the mouth of the Guadalquivir River.

Meanwhile, these soldiers, who were all pressed men and were leaving mistresses of long-standing and, by the way, the worst cutthroats in Andalusia, decided to try to make a fool of me.

When, for example, I said to them, "Down below, gentlemen, everyone below decks, it's nighttime, now," they would reply, "What do you think we are? Old hens, who spend all day in their nests? You leave us alone!"

I was so worried that I could not sleep thinking how I should ever see this voyage through. Except for fifteen sailors and six artillerymen, I had no one but sworn enemies aboard. So I thought up a way around the problem.

I carefully looked over these pressed men and picked out the biggest rogue of the lot, one whom the men seemed to respect. I then called him and said, "Ah, Señor Juan Gómez, come with me."

I took him into my cabin in the poop and asked him, "How long now have you served the king?"

"It must be five years now," he replied, "A while at Cádiz, then at Letrache after that, and I did one voyage with the fleet."

"Well," I replied, "I have taken a liking to you and I am only sorry that I can't promote you and have you as my lieutenant."

This delighted him, and he said, "There are men who would do worse than me."

"Well then," I went on, "if you would like to be sergeant of this company, go ashore now and make a formal application. And if you haven't enough money to buy yourself a halberd, I will pay for it myself."

"Thank you," he replied, "but I still have fifty *pesos* and will buy one myself, since your grace does me such great honor."

I must explain that there were men aboard who would have given two hundred silver dollars to go ashore. I gave him a letter for the purser and said, "Get along now. You have now put your foot on the ladder toward becoming a lieutenant. Remember now, I have put my trust in you."

He jumped into a longboat, went ashore, asked for his promotion, and came back in no time equipped with a sergeant's halberd.

When my cutthroats saw Gómez back as a sergeant, they thought that their schemes were even more certain of success. But I put my plan into operation and sent for the sergeant. When he came to my room, I said to him, "You are no longer the man you used to be. You are now an officer and for an officer, the slightest infractions of discipline are treason. Tell me, now, in your capacity as a sergeant, which of these men are the most dangerous and the most likely to cause us trouble."

"Do not disturb yourself, your grace," he replied, "they are a poor lot. Only Calderón and Montanes are near to being real men."

"All right," I said, "tonight, when we give the men orders to turn in, stand by me with a naked sword."

"But why, sir? By Christ, a truncheon is all they need."

"No, I say. When soldiers come to heel and eat their pride, it is not done with a big stick, but by a sword."

That evening, as usual, I said, "Down below, gentlemen, below decks. It's time for bed."

And Calderón and others replied with their usual insolence, "Let us alone!"

I was standing near Calderón, and I raised my sword and struck him with a powerful blow on the head and split it open so you could see his brains. Then I shouted, "Get down below, you insolent devils!"

In a moment, each one was in his bunk, gentle as a lamb.

Later, a man was sent to me, who said, "Sir, Calderón is dying."

"Let him confess his sins," I said, "and then throw him in the sea."

But I gave orders to my own crew that Calderón was to be looked after. Montanes I had clapped in irons, and the result of my plan was that these men were so quiet that for the whole voyage I scarcely heard a single "By Christ."

I must explain that I prevented swearing by making anyone who did so stand for an hour wearing on his head a great helmet weighing thirty pounds and a breastplate of the same weight.

I let the captain of the other ship know what I had done and recommended him to do the same. But when his men had heard what had happened on my galleon, they gave up all their plan of running the galleons ashore at Aranas Gordas and escaping and killing me if I tried to stop them.

CHAPTER
THIRTEEN

I sailed out of port and navigated for forty-six days with no sight of land, save the Canary Islands, until we reached Martinique. At Martinique, I took on stores of fresh water.

I saw some Indians there who, though they were quite wild, had grown accustomed to the comings and goings of our fleet and always used to come down to look at the ships. But, for all that, no one dared venture far ashore as the Indians were known to have captured many of our sailors and eaten them.

I then sailed north through the Virgin Islands. Not even savages lived there. Soon I made for the narrows of the Puerto Rico channel where English, Dutch, and French pirates used to cruise.

I arrived at the head of the channel after dark, but before risking the galleons I made a survey of the waters in a well-armed longboat.

During this reconnaissance, I left the galleons in one of the two excellent harbors there. I found no other ship in the channel so we sailed on to Puerto Rico. At sunrise, I was at the entrance to its harbor.

I sailed in, flags flying, and was enthusiastically welcomed by

Don Felipe de Biamonte y Navarra, the governor. He said to me, "It's a miracle you didn't meet the English pirate, Sir Walter Raleigh. He has been sailing around these waters with five ships, three large and two small ones, and has been robbing us every day."

Sir Walter Raleigh had gone to found a colony in South America, but had met with a series of misfortunes culminating in the loss of his son during a skirmish with the Spanish near the Spanish settlement of St. Thomas on the right bank of the Orinoco River.

Sir Walter's letters to his wife tell how heartbroken he was and that he was going straight home, feeling the expedition had been a failure. In the West Indies, he gave all his ships permission to part company with him and do as they liked. Presumably, the ship captured by Contreras was one of those that had accepted his offer.

Sir Walter returned home, and, shortly after, King James I of England had him executed. He was condemned to death on the charge of piracy, which had been based on complaints received from the Spanish government.

I unloaded the gunpowder, which they badly needed as their own stores had nearly run out, and also the fuses, lead, and some muskets. The governor, when he saw it all, was a happy man. He then asked me to leave forty men to reinforce his garrison. When the men heard of this there was a resistance such as I have never seen in my life. Nobody wanted to go ashore; they were almost in tears at the very thought of being left there. And not without reason, for to join the garrison there was equivalent to a life sentence in slavery. So I said to them, "My children, I am compelled to leave forty soldiers here, but I shall not order a single one of you ashore by name. You must condemn yourselves. Nobody, not even my servant, shall be exempt from the lottery. If he draws a black spot, he, too, will be left behind here."

I then made as many cards as I had soldiers and marked forty of them with black spots. I put them in a jar and mixed them all up in front of the men. Then, in order of the roll call, I summoned each man and said to him, "Draw a card. A black spot means that you stay in Puerto Rico."

They all did as I said, and the faces they made when they drew a black spot were worth seeing. However, since my servant, who also served as my barber, was the first to draw a black spot, proving the whole draw to be fair and above board, the unlucky ones consoled themselves.

The island of Santo Domingo was the court of the Spanish possessions in those parts at that time, and there was a president, law courts, and judges there. It was the first land that we Spaniards conquered in the Indies.

There were in Puerto Rico at that time two Spanish ships that were going to San Domingo. They were loaded with ox hides and ginger and, for safety, they sailed there in company with us. On my arrival, I was given a good welcome and set about carrying out the orders I had received in Spain. I was to set up a little fortress at the mouth of the river.

Two days later, I received word that Guaterral—that is what we called Sir Walter Raleigh—was riding at anchor with all his five ships not far away. I talked to the president about going to look for him, and he agreed to my plan. But the masters of the two cargo ships protested, saying, "If you lose our ships, you'll have to pay for them."

But for all that, I armed both of them, and another which had come from Cape Verde with a cargo of negroes. And with these ships and my own two galleons, we left port, trying to look as much like cargo ships as we could, and sailed towards the enemy.

When the enemy saw us, I veered away. But we fled very slowly and, in no time, our foes crowded in. Suddenly, I turned my bows on them, hoisted my standards, and attacked. They retaliated, and, since they could handle their sails better than we could, they were able to close in or open the range at their pleasure. I could not get my claws on them.

Still we fought. With a musket shot, we killed one of their captains before they sailed away, realizing that we were not merchantmen but warships after their blood.

I then sailed back to Santo Domingo to finish the fortress I was building. When I had completed it, I went on to Cuba, where I had to build another little redoubt. I did this in four days, posted a garrison of ten men there, and returned to Santo Domingo.

I left the merchantmen and fifty soldiers there and, taking only the other galleon with me, sailed for Santiago. Santiago was a town on the south side of Cuba. Havana, El Bayamo, and other cities had also been built on that island, but I do not remember all their names. I built another redoubt there and on leaving fell on a ship at anchor by the Isle of Pines. This ship surrendered without a fight. She turned out to be one of Guaterral's five. The English prisoners I took told me how Sir Walter Raleigh had fled and had made for the Bahama's channel. They also told me his son, who was a sea captain, too, had been killed, and thirteen men besides. Apparently, Sir Walter had sailed back to England, taking his prizes with him.

I sent word to the president of San Domingo and to the governor of Puerto Rico that Sir Walter Raleigh had left and they need not worry anymore.

The English ship I had captured was loaded with brazilwood and a small cargo of sugar, which the soldiers had looted. There were now twenty-one Englishmen aboard, all of whom I took to Havana, where they stayed until the arrival of the Spanish fleet, which, in due course, took them to Spain.

Meanwhile, I handed over all the stores and infantry I had to Señor Sancho de Alquiza, the captain general of Cuba and all the neighboring islands. I returned to Spain in the company of the Spanish fleet, under the command of Don Carlos de Ibarra. I went to the Indies in 1618 and got home to Spain in 1619.

† I SALVAGE SOME CANNONS †

I disembarked at Sanlúcar and was ordered to Seville. There I presented myself to Señor Juan Ruiz de Contreras, who was lying sick at the time. Before his illness, he had been fitting out a fleet to go to the Philippines. He told me that he had orders from the king that I was to help him. I did so, and Juan Ruiz sent me straightaway to Borgo, where six heavy galleons and two fleet tenders were being refitted. I carried out my orders and had the ships careened and caulked and then brought them from the careenage basin to Sanlúcar.

The ships were victualed, the artillery mounted, and the infantry—one thousand good men—as well as the sailors and artillerymen put aboard.

The general of the fleet was Don Çoaçola of the Order of Santiago, and he, like all his men, set sail with bad grace. And it was a bad end that they came to. Thirteen days after their departure from Cádiz in fine weather, they hit a storm. They were driven back and foundered only twenty miles from port.

The admiral was called something-or-other Figueroa; I do not remember his full name. However, after this disaster, he was wiped off the list of admirals and never was another fleet risked in his hands. I heard it said that without a doubt, it was the admiral's fault. He was no man of the sea. In fact, this was the first time he had been to sea.

The flagships of General Çoaçola and the admiral were both thrown up on the same beach. There was not a splinter of the general's ship left, and it was an eight hundred ton galleon with forty heavy-caliber cannons. The general and all his crew except for four men were drowned. The admiral's vessel had better luck. Almost every man was saved, as the ship hit the beach in deeper water and did not get smashed by the storm so quickly. The other ships ran with the storm through the straits; one of them was wrecked at Tarifa, another at Gibraltar, and a third at Cape Gata. The two fleet tenders were saved. And that was the end of that fleet.

In order to salvage what we could, I was sent off—just as though the disaster had all been my fault—with two schooners to the Tarifa beach to pick up the thirty bronze cannons that had been thrown ashore by the crew of the galleon. We had heard that two Algerian galleons were there waiting for a chance to capture the cannons, but up to then the crew ashore had stopped them. However, I arrived there with two schooners and took the cannons aboard. I had been given orders that if the enemy closed in on me and was likely to attack, I was to scuttle both the schooners with all the artillery aboard, so that the Algerian galleons should not capture these powerful guns and thus be as well armed as ourselves and a threat to our future.

I hugged the coast, while the Algerians stood out to sea. This maneuver came off most satisfactorily, as the Algerians were not able to attack in shallow water and I succeeded in saving the artillery.

† RELIEVE MÁMORA OR DIE FIGHTING †

A few days later, news reached Cádiz that Mámora was being besieged by land and sea—by land by thirty thousand Moors, who had made three assaults, and by sea by twenty-eight galleys, half of them Turkish and half Dutch. This enemy fleet was blockading the port and preventing any help arriving.

The duke of Medina gave orders that relief was to be sent immediately to Mámora. Don Fadrique de Toledo set about making his galleons fit for sea, but, due to one thing and another, he was unable to carry out the expedition. So we had to be satisfied with loading two schooners with gunpowder, fuses, and bullets.

The garrison at Mámora had scarcely anything left to fight with. As for fuses, they had even used the ropes that drew the buckets out of the wells and the cords that held up the soldiers' hammocks.

I realized how important it was for these two schooners to sail quickly, but I waited to see the result of the order to the garrison asking for volunteers. When neither officers nor men offered themselves, I went to the duke and said, "Señor, I request your excellency to entrust this expedition to me. If you will grant me this privilege of relieving Mámora, you may brand me on the forehead with an 'S' and a nail, as they do the slaves."

This pleased him very much, and he gave me orders to sail.

But when the captains of the garrison heard that I had been detailed for the expedition, they went to the duke and said, "This job should have been given to one of the officers under your grace's command and not to Contreras, who is only here to refit the fleet for the Philippines."

When I heard about this, I went into a public place and said loudly for everyone to hear, "By God, I asked for this command but have been given it only after those who insult me now have failed to come forward with their men when they had their orders. In any case, I am a captain and senior to the lot of them. And if anyone wants to repeat his words, I will wait for him by the church of Santa Caterina for a little throat cutting."

While I was walking toward the Santa Caterina Church, the duke's adjutant overtook me and told me that the duke wished to see me. I went to see him, and the duke told me to bring him a ticket of leave from Juan Ruiz de Contreras, under whose orders I was. I did this, and he gave me my sailing orders, which amounted to this: "With good luck, and with the help of God, relieve Mámora or die fighting."

CHAPTER
FOURTEEN

We have become accustomed to thinking of Contreras's battles with the Moors taking place in the Mediterranean on the North African coast, but this Mámora affair was on the Atlantic coast of Africa, in what is now Morocco.

I sailed, and planned my 130-mile route to Mámora so that at daybreak I would be in the middle of the enemy's fleet. The weather was perfect, and my timing worked precisely.

I reckoned that the twenty-eight enemy ships would be lying at anchor about three miles offshore so as to be out of artillery range. They would also be away from the surf and breakers set up by the sandbars across the mouth of the river; these breakers started nearly three miles out to sea. My plan was, then, at dawn to be in the middle of the fleet and to jump my schooner over the sandbar with the surf. If any of the enemy wanted to chase me, they would have to do the same, or try to sail around the sandbar and outflank me.

Well, everything went according to plan. When they saw me, all they did was to let fly a few musket shots and cannonballs, but nothing much. Everything happened so quickly that they had no time to do any damage.

I went into port. I was like the dove bringing the good news back to the Ark. The men welcomed me wildly and especially did good old Lechuga, the governor, who had been defending the town like the valiant man he was.

We put ashore the stores I had bought. Then, we saw the enemy ships weigh anchor and sail away. They were expecting the royal fleet to arrive, after seeing me, and they were not far wrong, as it did arrive the next morning.

That evening, I dined with the governor. While we were eating, we heard a trumpeter blow the alarm.

"What is it?" asked the governor.

"Six Moorish chiefs have come to discuss the price of peace," he was told.

The governor ordered the gates opened and these men taken to the house of a certain Jew, who used to act as interpreter. It was a custom for all these petty ambassadors to be taken to this Jew's house, as he arranged for them to have something to eat and smoke. When they were settled in with the Jew, Colonel Lechuga gave this order to his men, "All the powder and fuses are to be carried past the house where the chiefs are, and all of Captain Contreras's troops are to pass by the window also."

This was because my men were all well dressed, while the colonel's troops were in rags patched together with bits of leather. In this way, the colonel intended to make a good showing before the conference began.

The colonel and I then went to join these Moorish chiefs. They were men of quality, or so they seemed. They were wearing very finely embroidered sword belts, good quality boots, and excellent cloaks and fezzes. In fact, their clothes were altogether different from the local Moors. We each made our salutations. We then all sat down and drank to each other's health. These Moors, it turned out, were as heavy drinkers as the porters in Madrid!

The troops then started filing past the window carrying all the new stores, and then all my men marched past. The Moorish chiefs watched it all carefully and then one of them said, "We have just come to say good-bye to you. Seven thousand of our tribe are leaving this evening, and all the others will be on their way home during the night. We have come to see you to ask for your friendship and to ask if you would like to buy five hundred sheep and thirty cows."

"Certainly," said the governor, and gave them a great box of tobacco, tobacco being the most acceptable present one could possibly offer a Moor.

† A DIGRESSION INTO HISTORY †

Without being able to market their goods in Mámora, these Moors could not exist. They used to bring to Mámora everything they had looted and even things they had come by honestly. For four *reales,* they would give you a sheep as big as a heifer; for sixteen *reales,* a cow. Wheat could be had for three *reales,* and two chickens for a single *real.* So with the guarantee of the governor that they could still be friends and sell their goods in Mámora, the Moors went their way. I prepared for my departure, too.

This Mámora was situated on the mouth of a river. There was a sandbar, but, for all that, heavy galleons could still sail up the river. However, if the enemy captured it, they could do a great deal of damage to Spain, it being only 130 miles from Cádiz. Our ships were constantly going in and out of Cádiz and Sanlúcar.

At present, the Moors had to make the long journey from Algiers or Tunis, as well as pass through the dangerous Straits of Gibraltar. But if the Moors could make little sorties from Mámora, our ships would be in very great danger of being captured.

The Mámora River was navigable for ninety miles inland as far as Tleta. A whole fleet could be victualed and equipped there quite easily and cheaply. For that reason, the Dutch coveted it very much. A good example of what could happen if we lost Mámora could be seen from what went on at Salé, an excellent fortress some ten miles down the coast from Mámora.

At Salé, there was a little river that could only take shallow draft boats such as schooners and fleet tenders. Well, the Moriscos—they were the ones who had been thrown out of Andalusia—were continuously attacking the shipping on our Spanish coast with their nutshell boats. Every year, they captured some five hundred slaves from our ships arriving from the Azores, the Canaries, or from Brazil or Pernambuco. These pirates would make the voyage to the Portuguese coast and back in twenty-four hours, and make a little loot on the way. But you will be complaining by now that I am not telling my life story as I promised, but writing a history book. By God, though, I am not badly qualified to meddle in history.

† THE VICISSITUDES OF THE COURT †

That night, I sailed past the bar of the Mámora River and saw the dawn at Cádiz. At least, I tied up in the port before midday. I went to see the duke at Conil, and he invited me to lunch. With dessert, he read the letter which the governor of Mámora had given me to take to the king. The duke was delighted with the news and told me to leave for Madrid without wasting a minute.

He gave me a letter to the king, giving me full praise for my exploit, which made me very proud. To round off the honor, he gave me a purse containing a hundred doubloons. The duke's servants said that the duke was very pleased with himself as this expedition of mine was the neatest operation he had pulled off in his whole life.

I went to the Santa Maria Gate, where a contractor gave me 150 *escudos* to carry the post to Madrid. With that and good horses, I reached Madrid in three and a half days, a distance of well over two hundred miles. So, in all, I had left Spain, been to Barbary, come back, and gone to the court in under nine days.

I got off my horse at the palace and went up to see the king, dressed just as I was. Don Baltasar de Zúniga came out to meet me—may he rest in heaven—and I told him the news. He led me into the king's presence. I genuflected and gave him the two letters I was carrying, one from the governor of Mámora proving my story and the other from the duke.

Don Baltasar told the king that the governor of Mámora had referred them to Captain Contreras for a full story of what had happened. So the king gave the letters to Don Baltasar, and started asking me all about it. I told his majesty everything that he wanted to know, and, while I was answering all his questions, he played with and tossed about the cords and tassels which hung on the habit of the Religion I was wearing.

After a short time, Don Baltasar said, "Go and lie down, you must be worn out after your travels."

On my way downstairs, I passed by the offices of the government and the Council of State. The Council of State was in session at that time and, as I passed the door, an attendant asked me to go into the courtroom.

I went into the middle of the room and all the lords and gentlemen gave me a standing ovation. They asked me how things were in Mámora when I left. I told them my story and they were much relieved.

I then left and got on my post-horses and went to the house of an uncle I had at court. He was postmaster of Portugal. There I went to sleep; I needed it.

The next morning, a sergeant came to my house and told me that Don Baltasar wanted to see me. I went along, full of expectations. Although he was surrounded by many people who wanted to talk with him, he made way for me and immediately offered a chair. Then he asked me what posts I had previously held, adding, "Because his majesty wishes to do you a favor."

"I have been a captain of Spanish infantry," I replied, "and am

at the moment attached to the Philippine fleet and am picking up
the broken bits of it. My pay has been fifty *escudos* a month for the
last two years."

"What do you fancy?" he asked me. "What job catches your
eye?"

"I have not become too proud because of the services I have
done for the state, but the council did suggest to me yesterday
that I should be an admiral of some fleet or other."

"Jesus!" he replied. "Captain, you shall have it. And with a
pretty little salary, too!"

I kissed his hand for the honor he did me, and then he said,
"Go and see Secretary Juan de Ynástigui and he will give you
your new title."

I went home feeling very pleased. The next day, I went to see
this secretary. With him, I found Don Baltasar, who said to me,
"How is it going? Here is your commission and a draft of money.
But have patience for the rest. That is all his majesty can do for
you as regards your pay for the moment."

"Señor," I replied, "I don't need money if it is scarce. I am after
honor, not money."

I offered him back his draft, but he would not take it, though
he greatly appreciated my generosity. The draft was for three
hundred silver ducats.

The commission was a royal decree addressed to Don Fernando Carillo, president of the Indies. I took it to him, and he
received it with his usual heathen expression—he had no other—
and dryly dismissed me, saying, "His majesty's orders will be
dealt with in due course."

One month, then two months passed, and I was offered no
post, so I went to see Don Baltasar. He gave me a letter for Don
Fernando ordering that I should be given a post, adding that
since the king wished to do me a special favor, there was no need
to wait for the next sitting of the council.

I gave this letter to our good heathen, but he must have been
entangled with someone else. He had given away the only post

and I was left out in the cold. As soon as I learned this, I went, without wasting any more time, to beg an audience with the king. Anyone wishing for an audience with the king just had to wait in the corridors until the opportunity came to speak. When my chance came, I said, "Your majesty, I have served you for twenty-five years in many lands as you may see in this memorandum. My most recent service was carrying out the relief of Mámora. Your majesty honored me with a decree according me a post of admiral of a fleet. Many times before it has been suggested as a recompense for my services, but now after your majesty has actually given the instructions, the president has not yet put my name up."

He snatched the memorandum from my hands, swung himself round, and went off leaving us feeling all very uncomfortable. That Philip IV had only just come to the throne and was unused to his crown was the only explanation we could find for his behavior.

I went off to console myself with Don Baltasar and to ask his help again. While I was waiting in the anteroom, the president came in—the one with the heathen expression on his face that I have told you about. He was looking very bitter, as though he had been told off in high quarters. He went into Don Baltasar's office, and I followed in behind, despite the resistance of the doorman to whom I said, "It's quite all right, my lord president and I are on the same business."

Don Baltasar was there with the count of Monterey and a Dominican monk, the son of the count of Benavente. Don Baltasar was standing in the center of the room with the president when I went up to them and said, "I beg your excellencies to ask my lord president of the Indies if he is dissatisfied with me as an officer and for that reason will not give me a post."

The president stretched out his hands toward me and said, "Señor, you are an excellent officer. Did we not send you to Puerto Rico, where you acquitted yourself brilliantly?"

"If I am such an excellent officer, why has your lordship not appointed me to a post?" I asked. "The king has ordered it and his excellency, Don Baltasar, sent you a note to remind you."

"Señor," he said, "it will all be done, but for the moment there is no vacancy."

I turned to Don Baltasar and said, "Do not believe it, your excellency. He is deceiving you as he deceived me."

Then, the president shouted, "But I've told you all the posts are filled now."

Then Don Baltasar said, "But your excellency, please bear in mind that the king wishes to confer an honor on the captain."

Don Fernando could not speak. His words strangled in his throat, and he stormed out of the room. But before he reached the road he collapsed and fainted away.

He was put in his carriage for dead, but a doctor put tourniquets on his arms and legs to try to bring him back to life. By the grace of God, Don Fernando recovered sufficiently to make his confession. Then he died. May God forgive him the harm he did me. It was no satisfaction to me that he was without the breath of life, as I was still without the post of admiral. Don Baltasar then said to me, in effect, "It is not right for a favor to be conferred on a man who has killed the minister."

One might have thought I had let him have a volley from my culverin! However, as far as I have heard, it was not me who was to blame for his death, but a certain letter from very high quarters.

After all that, I retired from the palace completely. Then, one fine day, more than six months later, when I was least expecting anything, a sergeant came to call to tell me that the count of Olivares wanted to see me.

I went along, curious to see what it was all about. As I entered the room, the first thing he said was, "Captain Contreras, make no complaints to me, though I know you have been badly treated. The king has decided to build a fleet to guard the Straits of Gibraltar; I am to be the general of this fleet. The *junta* of the fleets has nominated sixteen practical and experienced men from various parts of the Spanish territories. Two have been chosen from the court: One is Colonel Don Pedro Osorio, the other is yourself. Consider it an honor."

I thanked his excellency for the favor that he had done me and said to him, "My lord, I have been a captain twice, but now I am earning fifty *escudos* a month from the fleet. I would not be happy to lead a company again at a lower pay."

"You have said enough," he said, "I will see that your pay is raised."

Then I replied, "Will your excellency permit me to raise this infantry company in Madrid?"

"It has never been done before," he said, "but if it will please you, I will speak to the king about it."

He got the king's permission and we raised our companies in Madrid, the colonel and I. We were the first officers ever to fly their own flags in Madrid while the court was there too.

CHAPTER FIFTEEN

† MY RUMORED DEATH †

I flew my standard in the Antón Martín quarter of the town and recruited 312 soldiers in less than a month. I paraded the men in front of all the nobility and marched out of Madrid at the head of the column.

My poor mother at last had some consolation for all the worries that my erratic career in this world had caused her.

The day after I had left Madrid, the rumor spread around the court that I had been killed at Getafe and the whole court was sad, just as though I had been a noble lord.

The marquis of Barcarrota was said to have started the story about my death at a *pelota* game. Immediately, the president of Castille, Don Francisco de Contreras, rushed off horsemen to find out the facts and to arrest my murderer, if the story turned out to be true.

I sent back word by the horsemen that I was well, and the court was delighted. Now this next thing I will tell you shows the advantage of being well thought of by the world. This rumored death earned me five hundred masses, which the kind people at the hospice of Buen Suceso had celebrated for the repose of my soul. And offerings for the saying of three hundred more were received. I learned all this much later from Don Diego de Córdoba, who was majordomo of the hospice.

† AN UNFORTUNATE NAVAL ACTION †

I went on with my troops to Cádiz, and made an impressive entry into the town at the head of my three hundred or so men.

We were assigned to serve with the fleet and embarked to go to Gibraltar to join the ships, which were under the command of General Don Juan Fajardo. The whole fleet consisted of twenty-two big galleons and two fleet tenders. At Gibraltar, we were assigned to a galleon called *The Admiral of Naples*. This galleon was so called as she was from Naples and belonged to the duke of Ossuna. She was one of the six galleons in our squadron, which had been made famous by the élan and courage of General Francisco de Ribera. If only it had pleased God to make stalwart Ribera general of the whole fleet and not commander only of his six galleons, the king would have been served better and we would have won some glory.

Some Turkish ships were sighted going through the Straits of Gibraltar and along the African coast under our very noses. We sallied out with a few ships and succeeded in capturing some of them.

A little later, on 6 October 1624, we had an encounter with eighty-two ships of the Dutch fleet. Not all of that fleet, however, were men-of-war. We ran them down about fifty miles to sea from Málaga. All that I can tell you is that Ribera's flagship and my ship, which was second in importance in our Neapolitan fleet to the flagship of Don Juan Fajardo, attacked the enemy at four o'clock in the afternoon.

I will tell you no more of what happened after that than that the enemy laughed us to scorn. If Ribera's ship had not been holed below the waterline, and if he had not had to stop and lower a boat and repair it, the battle might have turned out better.

Well, as for this regrettable cannonball, all I will say is that it was not fired by any of the enemy ships. Let no more be said and let us pass on.

Night fell and our Dutchmen sailed through the straits without being challenged by a soul. That was more than they had ever hoped for, and I heard later that they had been prepared to lose as many as one-quarter of their ships.

† THE ENGLISH ATTACK CÁDIZ †

We sailed back into Gibraltar and Don Juan Fajardo stayed there, while Ribera and I went off to meet the galleons coming from the Americas with silver. We found them and escorted them as far as Sanlúcar. On this voyage, we captured two Turkish ships loaded with sugar.

We returned to Gibraltar to spend the winter, and there I fell sick. Don Juan Fajardo allowed me twenty days convalescence in Seville and, when I overstayed my leave, gave my company to another officer. When I heard this I went to the court to submit my complaint, and there his majesty gave me the command of five hundred foot soldiers, divided into four companies for service in the Genoese galleys.

I recruited the men, and we were just about to set off for Genoa when I received orders to go to Lisbon with all my men to man the fleet. It had just been equipped to combat the English. Thomás de Larraspur was in command.

We waited for over two months for this English fleet, first at Cascaes, then at Balém. We had gotten rumors that they were going to attack us at Lisbon and that the Jews there had sent for them.

The English learned that we were waiting for them near Lisbon, so they swept round onto Cádiz. But even when this was known, we were ordered to keep our guard on Lisbon, and we did so until we heard that the fleet had retreated to England.

† LOPE DE VEGA BEFRIENDS ME †

The marquis of La Hinojosa, the supreme commander on land and sea, then set about demobilizing his forces; my company was among the first to be dismissed.

We went back to Madrid to ask for orders to join the Genoese galleys for which my company was originally recruited. But that fine flame of hope flickered and went out. The truth was that the Genoese had become strong and no longer needed Spanish troops. And despite the efforts of the duke of Tarsis in trying to keep the galleys manned by Spaniards, he never succeeded. And so there we were, in Madrid, unemployed and always asking to go on service.

For all that, I was not so unlucky. Lope de Vega, a man to whom I had never spoken a word in my life, took me to his house and said most gracefully, "Sir, with men such as yourself, one is compelled to share one's cape."

He then kept me with him as his companion for more than eight months. He gave me my meals, a bed, and even made me presents of clothes. May God be kind to him! As though what he had done was not enough, he dedicated a comedy, *King Without a Kingdom,* to me. It was in the twentieth volume of his works and was about my being accused of being king of the Moriscos.

Having no money, I felt ashamed of living at the court, which at the best of times was no place for a soldier. I decided to go back to Malta to see if I had any expectations from the order and if I could earn a meal there.

I asked the council for some pay to go to Sicily, it being near Malta. I was given thirty *escudos,* which was five *escudos* more than they usually give to captains. When everything was in order, I set out for Barcelona and, by way of Genoa and Naples, reached Sicily. There I presented my papers and got another pay.

Contreras, it seems, realized only much later what an honor Lope de Vega had done him by his prolonged hospitality. In fact, only when Contreras saw his host's plays being performed in a Madrid theater did he learn how important a man de Vega was. However, to the exceedingly civilized Lope de Vega, this bear of a man telling fantastic stories of his exploits and his amours must have been a great amusement. On the other hand, there is little doubt that de Vega much respected him. The dedication to Contreras is long and enthusiastic, detailing all the battles Contreras fought in the name of God and his country.

The two of them had another bond: both were of the Order of St. John. Lope de Vega was a knight of justice and Contreras, at that time, was a brother servant-at-arms.

† I AM GOVERNOR OF PANTELLERIA †

A month later, when I went to the viceroy of Sicily, the duke of Albuquerque, to ask permission to go to Malta, he offered me the governorship of Pantellaria, an island which lay almost on the Barbary Coast. There was a small castle there and a garrison of 120 Spanish soldiers.

On my way to Pantellaria, I passed through Malta and made inquiries about getting a commandery, on the income of which I could live. But I was told that I had not done enough service for the order, nor had I even lived in Malta long enough to earn any privileges. In any case, the commanderies which were given to ordinary brothers servants-at-arms were not many, and the best of them did not have an income of six hundred ducats.

I was governor of Pantelleria for nearly a year and a half. During that time, all that happened was that I had a few quarrels with those who came there to victual their ships with meat and water.

But what I did do was set about putting the church in order. It belonged to the Brotherhood of Our Lady of the Rosary and was as badly thatched as a roadside inn.

I sent to Sicily for wood and paints and for a painter. I had a new wood roof made, supported on good strong beams, with six stone vaultings to further support it. I also had a sacristy and a pulpit built. Then, I had the whole church painted, the roof, the sanctuary—where there were, you must imagine, four pictures of the four evangelists—and the wooden altar of Our Lady. On top of the main vaulting, a fresco of God the Father appeared, and down each side of this arc the "fifteen mysteries" were portrayed.

With the following conditions, I endowed the church with an income in perpetuity: A sung high mass had to be celebrated during Carnival time every year, with a deacon and subdeacon, and with a catafalque draped in black cloth and surrounded with candles. A dozen low masses had to be said as well. And for vespers, the office for the dead had to be sung. All the masses and offices were to be dedicated to the souls in purgatory. Over and above that, I put funds at the disposal of the church for two hundred masses to be said as soon as news of my death was received; these were to be dedicated to the repose of my soul.

I also left some money so that the pictures could be cleaned every two years and the church whitewashed. I also instituted a monthly low mass for the repose of my soul. I had seen to it that the church was the most beautiful thing on the island, and I saw to it that the masses had equal splendor.

Having finally adorned the church as beautifully and expensively as I could, I asked leave of the duke of Albuquerque to go to Rome. He grudgingly granted me four months to go and come back in. I sailed for Palermo and there embarked on a ship bound for Naples, from where I went by road to Rome.

† HIS HOLINESS HONORS ME †

At Rome, I set about finding ways and means around the rules of service and residence which the Religion insisted one had to fulfill before one could be granted a commandery. I prepared a memorandum and submitted it to his holiness, Urban VIII. He rejected it so quickly that I resolved to speak to him myself about it.

He granted me an audience, and I told him of all the services I had done the church. Then I added, "For whom are the treasures of the church, if they are not for men like me, who have grown old fighting to defend the Catholic faith?"

Then his holiness, being moved by my deeds and my Christian zeal, not only gave me a brief for the grand master exempting me from the legalities of residence and service, but even gave me another brief commanding the Order of St. John to receive me as a knight. I was to enjoy the privileges of seniority and the right to any honors and commanderies normally only accorded to knights of justice, all of whom were of noble blood. Then, over and above that, his holiness conceded a perpetually indulgenced altar to my church on Pantellaria and this privilege was attached to my personal altar for seven years, with no more than a need for three masses to be said yearly for a plenary indulgence.

I was very satisfied, but I did not rest until I had gotten my privileges in writing from the monsignori who were his holiness's ministers for these matters. They thought his holiness had been overgenerous—it was true that there was no precedent for such lavishness—so they hedged around my privileges with a thousand little snags, but they were all brushed aside when the count of Monterey and his wife, the countess, wrote to the monsignori. If it had not been for them, I should have gotten nothing worth having. He was at that time Spanish ambassador extraordinary to Rome.

Having wound up my affairs, I made my plans to go back to Malta and to Palermo to get the pay that had fallen due to me while I was away. I went to beg leave of his excellency the count of Monterey, but he ordered me not to leave Rome, saying that he would have need of me. So I stayed. The count was very pleased that I had obeyed him and ordered his treasurer to pay me thirty *escudos* a month, which he did with complete punctuality.

After six months, I again asked his excellency leave to go to present my briefs at Malta. He allowed me two months to go and come back in. I left Rome and went to Malta by way of Naples and Sicily. I presented my papal briefs, and the orders were carried out on the spot. I was knighted with all due solemnity. The bull was issued by the grand master, and he gave it to me himself. I was more proud than if I had been born the Infante Carlos. It read, "By reason of his great prowess and fine deeds, Captain Contreras is armed knight. He will have a right to all the command-eries and honors of the order customary to knights of justice."

That day, we had a great banquet to celebrate my honors. But next morning, I left for Rome and was back there in no time. My whole journey took only thirty-four days, including my stay in Malta and receiving my knighthood, though I covered nearly nine hundred miles. At Rome, I straightaway went to kiss the hands of the count and countess, and they were delighted to see me back so soon with my new honors.

† THREE CARDINALS COME TO ROME †

Eight days later, the count sent me off with two of his big country coaches, each drawn by six horses, to welcome Cardinal Sandoval, Cardinal Espínola, and Cardinal Albornoz. They had just come from Spain by ship and were landing at Palo, twenty miles from Rome.

He instructed me to invite them to come to stay at his house and to tell them that everything had been prepared to accommodate them in a style befitting their dignity. I arrived at Palo and found their eminences staying at the castle. I said my piece, and they were charmed but replied, "These are the dog days, and we couldn't think of living in Rome in such hot weather. We shall stay in the nearby hills."

Seeing that they had made up their minds, I asked them to reconsider their plans and suggested that they put their service to their king first. Only then did they decide to risk their health.

Two hours after dark, I had all the horses harnessed and all their seventeen coaches loaded. My three milord cardinals traveled in one of the count's coaches, and I, with their chamberlains, in the other. Then to make sure that milord cardinals were not incommoded by the heat of the sun, I led off at such a speed that we reached Rome at dawn.

My cardinals settled into the ambassador's palace, each with his own apartment, and living with his own chamberlain and servants. They had all the pomp, circumstance, and delicacy that you can imagine.

They were lavishly entertained by the count for a month, while waiting for houses to be gotten ready for them, and they were visited by all the college of cardinals.

Having delivered the cardinals to the count, I returned to my inn, where I still am at the time of this writing, and where I shall stay until I receive new orders from his excellency. My only desire is to serve him well.

There is one thing that I hold to be a miracle. It was that those milords came into Rome on St. Peter's Day, when the dog days are at their most murderous. Not a single one of their three hundred servants died. As for their eminences, they did not even suffer from a headache. All I can assume is that this talk about dog days is so much folderol. It is true, though, that I recommended them at Palo to stay out of the sun, to keep their windows closed and, above all, to avoid changes of temperature by not moving about too much.

What you have read now is what has happened to me up to today, 11 October 1630. Without a shadow of a doubt, I have forgotten hundreds of things, but how can one, in eleven days, remember and write down all the memories, happenings, and adventures of thirty-three years?

Well, there it is: my life, unadorned and as naked as it came from the hands of God, without flourishes and without fine speeches. It is the truth and that is all I can say. Christ be praised!

CHAPTER SIXTEEN

Shortly after, the marquis of Cadreyta passed through Rome. He was on his way to Germany, where he was to be Spanish ambassador, though at the time he was still holding the post of ambassador to her serene highness, the queen of Hungary.

The count decided to entertain him and sent me to meet him and to invite him to come and stay as the count's guest. Unfortunately, he was not carrying his papers of credit from the queen and for that reason his holiness would not have been able to give him an audience in his capacity as an ambassador, so I took him outside Rome to Frascati, the town of easy and luxurious living, where he waited until he could get new orders.

When the marquis got them, he moved into Rome and stayed with the count, where he was entertained royally. He kissed the pope's foot, made and received all his diplomatic visits, and then left for Ancona, where he joined the queen of Hungary. Together they returned to the imperial court.

Only then did he go to take up his post of ambassador to Germany. His stay in Rome was glittering and extravagant, just what one would expect of such a grandee.

The next thing to happen was that the count sent me off to borrow a galley from the countess of Tarsis, as he wanted to send me and his secretary, Juan Pablo Bonete, to Madrid to deal with some urgent private matters of his. We got the galley, embarked, and in no time we were in Barcelona. I was ordered to make posthaste to Madrid, which I did, and the count's business was dispatched in as short a time as he could have hoped.

I stayed in Madrid more than two months—that was in 1631— and I thoroughly enjoyed seeing Lope de Vega's delightful comedies. Without a doubt, Lope de Vega is the phoenix of Spain, eminent in everything he touches. Anybody who memorizes his works seems to become a dramatic poet himself. He alone would have been enough to bring honor to Spain and to cast his shadow on all the nations of the world.

† VESUVIUS ERUPTS †

From Madrid, I went to Naples, where the count of Monterey had just become viceroy. On my arrival, I was ordered to take command of a company of Spanish infantry.

"I have been a captain of infantry four times before, sir," I complained to the count. But he stuck to his guns, and I took the company and we became the viceroy's bodyguard. Two months later, we were sent to garrison the town of Nola.

One quiet morning—Tuesday, 16 December—at dawn, Mount Nola, which is also called Vesuvius, let off an immense cloud of smoke. As the day advanced, the sun was hidden. There were rumblings, and ashes rained on us. We, at Nola, were just at the bottom of the volcano, four miles away at the most. When the local people saw day turn into night and saw the rain of ashes, they became frightened and began to evacuate.

That night was terrifying. The Day of Judgment may be worse, but I cannot imagine it.

It rained ashes, then clods of earth, then balls of fire. It was just like the burning slag that blacksmiths take out of their furnaces. Mostly, these balls of fire were as big as a fist, but some were even bigger. Then the earth shook; twenty-seven houses crumbled that night. I listened to the noise of the cypresses and the orange trees being uprooted and rent in two as though by some gigantic ax. Terror was in all our hearts, and everyone was crying and moaning.

On Wednesday, there was scarcely any daylight and we had to go about with candles. I scoured the countryside with a squadron of soldiers and found some flour. I had seven loads brought back to Nola and set the men baking bread to feed those who were homeless or who had left their homes for fear of their collapsing.

There were two convents of nuns there, who would not leave, although the vicar had given them permission to do so before he himself left. These two convents collapsed, but with no harm to the nuns, as they were in the body of the church praying to God.

Meanwhile, my troops made up their minds to mutiny. They decided to come to me and to force me to leave Nola, as the lava was approaching us. On their way to visit me, I met them all, by chance, on the road. When I came up to them I said, "Where are you off to, gentlemen?"

"Sir . . ." said one of them, but before he could say any more, I said, "Gentlemen, anyone who wants to leave may. As for myself, I shall not leave till my heels are burnt. When that time comes, since our flag isn't heavy, I'll carry it myself."

No one said a word.

That day, we spent half in the dark, half in twilight. We shall never know all the miseries that went on. Many had not fled. Women with their hair and clothes awry strayed aimlessly and children were lost, not knowing where next to go. Here, two houses collapsed, there another caught fire. Then night fell. The next morning, it was impossible to escape, because of the hail of ashes. The volcano went on burning continuously, and the rain of cinders did not let up. Then streams of lava started pouring down the mountainside. The noise alone was enough to strike terror in everyone. One of the streams was coming toward Nola, so I chose thirty men, some my soldiers, others locals, and with picks and shovels we dug a trench and turned the lava stream against two little villages. The lava stream carried these hamlets away and all the cattle, just like a swarm of ants moving a house. We could not save anything.

While I was watching this happen, I could not help thinking that if I had left when my soldiers had wanted me to the town of Nola would have been drowned in lava.

On Friday, God gave us rain. It was a mixture of cinders and water, which made a sort of cement which was so hard that one could not even break it with a pickax. Real rain, instead of a rain of burning cinders, gave us a little encouragement.

On the Saturday, the church's walls cracked. Then the barracks collapsed. No one was hurt, as all the soldiers preferred to risk the cinders than trust the barracks, but an earthquake shook everything around like water sluiced from side to side in one's mouth.

On the Sunday, we got orders from the count. He had believed us all to be dead, as he had not been able to get word through. However, he ordered us to retire to Capua.

I was very unhappy about leaving the nuns, as I felt sure they would lose their courage when they saw me go. But it was advisable for me to obey orders because if there were any serious mishaps after I had been told to retire the blame would have been thrown on my shoulders.

I left with nothing more than what I was wearing. Even if I had wanted to take a trunk, there was no way of carrying it.

We arrived at Cápua looking such a sight that people swore we looked like men coming back from working in hell. Most of us were without shoes, and our clothes and skins were half-burnt. In a week there, we put ourselves to rights and then we celebrated Christmas happily, although we knew that Vesuvius was still pouring out its lava.

† THREAT AND COUNTERTHREAT †

After a week, we got orders from the count to go and stay in Casales, a town close by. While we were there, we got back some of the things we had lost at Nola. I myself got back two chests full of clothes, which was all that was left of my possessions, but it was a miracle that I even got those.

At Casales, I discovered one of the wickedest tricks in the world being played against the poor people of the town. This is how it worked.

The rich people who had big houses and could afford to have troops billeted on them had one of their sons take deacon's orders in the church. Then, they would make over all their possessions into his name and, in that way, were relieved of the duty of having to accept troops. The archbishop took their side, as they helped maintain him. I explained the trickery to the bishop, and he replied, "It's within the law, you know."

I got indignant and ordered my men out of the houses of the poor and into the houses of the rich. I asked each house, "Which room belongs to the man in orders?"

"That one," they would reply.

"Respect it like the Day of the Lord," I would say to my men, "and these others, who lives in them?"

"Sir," they would reply, "his father, his mother, his sisters, and his brothers."

Once they had admitted that, I used to billet three or four soldiers on them.

These rich people went off to complain to the archbishop, and I received a letter from him saying, "Be careful what you do, or you will be excommunicated."

When I read it, I laughed out loud. Then one of these savage clerics—they were called savage in those parts because they were only in minor orders and were often married—got on his mare to go and tell the archbishop how his letter had been received. One of my soldiers, seeing him make off, grabbed the horse's bridle and reins and said to him, "You wait here until I have spoken to the captain."

But the mare did not understand the reins any better than her master understood Latin and she reared up and threw the cleric on the ground. However, shaken as he was, he went and laid his complaint in front of the archbishop, who wrote back to me, "You are excommunicated by virtue of chapter *quisquis pariente del diablo.*"

"You, too, be careful what you do," I replied in a message to him. "I don't understand this *quisquis* business, and, as for being any relative of the devil, I am not. Nor is he anywhere in my family tree. Now you beware, if I get myself excommunicated no one will be safe from me unless he is on the moon. For that very purpose, God gave me ten fingers and five hundred Spanish veterans."

The archbishop received my letter, but he did not reply to it. What he did do, however, was to write to those who had complained to him advising them to put the case to the viceroy, as he himself was also doing, and to ask the viceroy to have me removed as there seemed to be nothing else they could do.

They set to work with a will, but during the forty days while they waited for my removal, I made the rich pay up and none of the poor suffered.

† I BECOME GOVERNOR OF AQUILA †

After these forty days, I was appointed governor of Aquila and given orders to march there immediately with my troops. Aquila was one of the largest cities in the kingdom of Naples. In my orders, I was told that the bishop was no longer respected there and that the people were threatening to kill him. I was told to punish the offenders.

This city of Aquila was ill disciplined. The Aquilans scarcely acknowledged the kingdom, mainly because it was on the borders of Romagna, and because it was as far from Naples as it could be.

On 9 February, I set out. We crossed the Five Mile Plain through three feet of snow. I had a fine time keeping the soldiers going.

I took all my five hundred hard-bitten Spaniards with me, and we entered the town in skirmishing order. I announced myself civil governor and military governor and then arrested as many of the rebels as I could, before they fled.

I billeted my buccaneers in the houses of the rebels, which was a most effective plan. I proclaimed that no one could enter or leave the town carrying firearms. Since these Aquilans carried guns as naturally as they wore hats, it was a miracle that they all obeyed me. But it may have been something to do with my billeting system.

Then, one day, six servants of the count of Claramonte arrived at the Naples gate well armed with muskets and pistols. The count was then the governor of the province. These men all had very long hair—what we called a Nazarene haircut—and it was the style adopted by all the brigands and highwaymen in those parts. The guard at the gate told them that they could not enter the city ·without the military governor's permission.

"Military governor?" they said. "Never heard of such a person."

My guard at the Naples gate consisted of only four men, and, since two of them were having their dinner, my long-haired friends forced their way into the town and swaggered around the marketplace not expecting any more harm to be done to them than in the past.

When all this was reported to me, I ordered all the city's gates to be closed and, with eight soldiers, went out to arrest them. I found them trying to look as innocent as lambs. When I attacked them, they fought back, but I surrounded them and captured them with the loss of only one of my men wounded.

I then tried and condemned these ruffians. I gave them two hours' respite and then carried out the sentence I had given them. It was that their hair should be cut off and for evermore they were to wear it short, and that they were each to receive two hundred lashes of the whip seated on a donkey, in the old Spanish style.

This punishment was carried out very well by the executioner, although neither he nor anyone in Aquila had ever seen or done anything like it before. I then had these ruffians taken off their donkeys and, in the way I used to do it in the galleys, had them washed in saltwater and vinegar. The next day, I sent them off to Naples to serve six years as galley slaves.

When the news of my summary justice reached the governor of the province, he could not believe his ears. He had the news verified and then wrote me, "By virtue of what authority have you done this?"

"I have condemned these men," I replied, "in my capacity as military governor."

"I am the only governor in this province," he wrote me.

"Go and complain to the count of Monterey," I replied. "He gave me my orders."

This annoyed him, and he decided to come to Aquila to arrest me. He assembled three hundred cavalry and a few infantry, but when I got warning I wrote him, "Will your Lordship take great care not to encourage the whole country to rebel? It is already mutinous, and it was to put down these rebels that I was sent here. I beg you as a minister of the crown not to start up a shameful civil war without first referring to the viceroy, the count of Monterey. If I have misbehaved, he will punish me."

But he paid no attention to my letter and went on his same course. When I got the next reports from my spies, I saw that it was going to be a very serious matter. So I picked one hundred of my five hundred men, provisioned them well with gunpowder, shot, and fuses and put two pistols in my charger's saddle holsters.

I took with me also two thousand *escudos* in doubloons for safety's sake and went to meet the count. I stopped overnight at a village, and from there I wrote him a letter in which I said, "Since you treat the king's service so lightly, go your own road. But take a good horse, for, if I catch you, I swear by Christ I will have you whipped like the others."

I would have done it, and much better than I described it to him, too. I was sure I could beat his rabble of soldiers and once done, I would have ridden off to Rome and then to Milan and Flanders, where nothing would have been heard of the business. As it was, it was easy enough for me to escape to the papal states, which were only a six-hour ride away.

However, the Claramonte read my letter and sent it to the viceroy. He retreated to his own lands and I to mine.

The next day, I heard that there was a highwayman ranging the countryside, robbing the farmers and the convents. That day, I came to the little village where he was. I found him sleeping, thinking himself as safe as the king in Madrid. I gave him a rousing awakening, and he leapt out of his bed and through the window into the garden. But my troops jumped as well as he did, and they caught him. We tied him up and took him back to Aquila. The Aquilans were astonished to see him caught at last, as they thought that there was no one who would risk his neck trying to capture him. I locked him up in the castle, tried him, condemned him to death, and gave him two days of grace.

During these two days, I had a scaffold built in the marketplace and a large executing sword forged. The Aquilans scoffed when they saw the scaffolding go up and laughed when they were told for whom it was intended. But they had great big round eyes when they saw him without his head five days later at three o'clock in the afternoon.

I paid the executioner ten *escudos* and gave him one of my suits.
But he was an unpractised executioner. He was rather like those
doctors who learn their surgery in hospitals at the expense
of innocent people—not that the highwayman was innocent,
he was quite the opposite. He was called Jácomo Ribera, a native
of Aquila, and everybody knew him, or at least had heard his
name.

† I IMPRISON THE RED CLOAKS †

I was at Aquila for Easter Day. And, at that time, the councillors
and the officials who dealt with fixing the market prices were very
angry with me as I was making their speculations difficult. On
Holy Thursday, I ordered them to communicate as I was doing,
but out of sheer malice they refused. Then, to annoy me further
they would not attend the Easter Sunday mass with me in their
official capacities but stayed in the city council chambers.

Easter Sunday came, and the bishop celebrated a pontifical
high mass. I waited for the councillors until the mass started and
then went in to take my seat along with my clerk. This clerk, by
the way, would never sign any of the warrants for the punishment
that I have already told you about. But I was not alarmed about it,
as he was a local man and had to stay on when I had gone.

I must explain a custom of Aquila. There were five councillors
and each had two red-cloaked attendants, paid for out of the
city's funds. No councillor would leave his house or go anywhere,
even if it were a matter of life or death, without his attendants.

When I saw myself alone at this pontifical high mass, I knew
that these rogues were up to their tricks. I called my sergeant to
my seat and said, "Go and arrest all the councillors' attendants,
and in each of the councillor's houses billet six soldiers, with
orders to eat everything they can find in the house and in the

kitchen. They are to respect the women but not leave the houses until further orders."

This order was carried out most enthusiastically by my Spaniards, who had no good dinner to look forward to in their present lodgings.

When the councillors heard that I had arrested all their red-cloaked attendants, they were furious, but could not go out into the streets. They sent me messages even by the hand of gentlemen of the town, but I always replied, "Come and see me yourselves."

But they just stayed where they were, which was where the sergeant had arrested their attendants.

The bishop begged me to order my soldiers out of the houses and to release the attendants so that the councillors could go home. I agreed to the first request on the condition that each soldier was given three testoons, which was equal to nine *reales*. The councillors paid up in a second. By God, they would have paid up three hundred ducats not to have my soldiers living with them. I fear they did not love us. But, for all that, these soldiers and their friends—with their nine *reales* and a huge dinner—had a better Easter than the councillors, who spent it where their servants were arrested. They stayed there like that, so as not to break the city's custom and so as not to lose the privilege of having attendants.

The bishop pressed me to free the red-cloaked attendants so that the councillors could go home. My reply to him was, "I only arrested their men so that there should be no embarrassment about precedence and about who should carry my cushion in the church. However, if each councillor would kindly pay a ducat to the Convent of Penitents, I shall be pleased to free their attendants.

They paid up like lightning so as to get out of the sort of magic circle they were in. It was nothing less; they were free but could not move a step.

I had a few other little contretemps with these councillors. They raised the price of meat, fish, and bread to far too high a price, and arranged that the merchants supply their households free with meat and fish, while the baker made a cash payment to them.

When I learned about this game, I asked them to invite me to their next tax and price-fixing meeting, and they did so. When they were deciding on the prices, I said, "But gentlemen, don't you think it a pity to fix the prices so low? These things are worth more, and if prices are higher there will be much more on sale in the markets."

They saw the heavens opening and pushed the tax and the prices up higher and higher. The figures were finally fixed, and then I said to them, "My household is large, but as a knight of Malta, a captain of infantry, and as a military governor and civil governor, I am exempt from these taxes. Nevertheless, I want to be the first to pay them. And you, gentlemen, must buy provisions in proportion to the size of your households and pay cash, just as I shall."

I then turned to the shopkeepers who were there and said, "I swear by God that if you make a single present of an ounce of anything to any of these gentlemen, I shall have you flogged."

The shopkeepers, knowing my reputation, realized that I was in earnest and submitted.

One of the councillors then said, "But, sir, we never eat fish in our house."

"That doesn't matter a bit," I said, "I want you to eat fish, and I want you to enjoy the fixed prices and the taxes as I and all the poor people of the town do."

The end of that was that the prices all came down by over a half on everything.

To go back to our governor, the Claramonte, he had dispatched the letter I had written him to the count of Monterey. The viceroy decided on that evidence, and the complaints of the councillors at Aquila, to relieve me of my governorship. But both the Claramonte and I were sacked on the same day. Monterey gave me, before my departure from Aquila, the command of a squadron of heavy cavalry, but to the Claramonte he gave nothing at all. And so ended my governorship of Aquila, which lasted three months and seven days.

CHAPTER SEVENTEEN

† NEAPOLITAN FESTA †

I left Aquila to take command of my squadron of cavalry at Naples. I found it encamped at Cápua, but had to order them down to Naples to have them officially handed over to me by the general of cavalry, Don Gaspar de Acevedo.

On the same day that the general handed the squadron over to me in the presence of Quartermaster Concubilete, a complete check of the horses was made. The squadron had previously been commanded by Don Hector Piñatelo, who had just been promoted to the post of adjutant to Don Gaspar, and who was also present at this handing over.

When the cavalrymen were given back their horses after the inventory, one of them shouted, "My horse has been changed!"

Then many others shouted the same thing. So I went up to Don Hector Piñatelo and said, "Your horse belongs to the company. And the troopers say that your grace has left us a lot of tired horses and kept the best ones for himself."

"It is quite untrue," he replied, "I have not taken a single horse."

Among Italians, such a remark as mine was not taken as an

insult, but I had to maintain my reputation in front of my Spanish troops. I raised my hand, took hold of his pointed beard, and tugged it hard.

Don Hector Piñatelo dropped his cane and drew his sword in a flash. I was not slow in drawing mine either. We fought, but no blood was drawn, as the crowd closed in and we could not get at each other properly. One unfortunate German in the viceroy's bodyguard paid the piper. He might as well have had the pleasure of tugging Piñatelo's beard, as he got a slash across the cheek by mistake.

Don Gaspar de Acevedo stopped the fight, and we were put under house arrest for three days. When the count had gotten the reports of the prince of Asculi's and the colonel, he ordered us to come to his antechamber to make friends again. Don Hector Piñatelo had the prince of La Rochela, and I, Don Gaspar de Acevedo as witnesses for this reconciliation. After that, we were both still very wary of each other, or, as the buccaneers say, "We kept our eyes peeled."

So I became a cavalry captain. This brought me new things to think about. The count instructed me to arrange a parade of all the Spanish and Italian cavalry and infantry in the kingdom of Naples. The whole cavalry, including the recent levies, was more than 2,500 horsemen. We had so many infantrymen that we did not need to parade the irregular levies. The 2,700 Spaniards and the 8,000 Italians—all regulars—made a fine enough sight by themselves, every one of them being a picked man.

What a grand sight we made that day! Even I, a poor man, wore the count's colors. I had two trumpeters and four attendants, all dressed in silver-braided scarlet uniforms, with gilded swords, plumes, and cloaks to match. I had five horses, two of them having silver-braided coverings, all of them with saddle holsters and ornate pistols in them. We were displaying our colors of azure blue with silver flames. I was wearing chamois boots braided with silver lace and collars and cuffs in the same style.

On my helmet, I had a mountain of blue, green, and white plumes and on my shoulders a gold-embroidered cloak that was so big it would have done as a bedspread.

Like this, then, we entered the main square of Naples—myself at the head, followed by my sergeant major and standard and eighty well-armed cavalrymen, wearing scarlet cloaks. My brother, who was my lieutenant, brought up the rear. It was magnificent. I will leave you to imagine the applause we received.

Myself and all the other captains rode or marched our companies past the palace where the count of Monterey with their eminences Cardinals Sabeli and Sandoval were watching. From another balcony, the countess of Monterey and her ladyship the marchioness of Monterroso, with their ladies-in-waiting, were also watching.

As each squadron of cavalry passed the count, it made a caracole and dipped its flags; the infantry just made their salute by lowering their standard. Then we all passed on toward the castle, where we paraded in a body.

After that, we had a sham battle. The skirmish between the infantry and the cavalry was a thing worth seeing. By this time, their excellencies were going to the Castel Nuovo with the cardinals, and we gave them a full artillery salute, which was so realistically warlike that one could scarcely believe there were no cannonballs.

But how could anything go wrong? Our viceroy seemed to know precisely how and when everything should be done, just as though he were the oldest of old campaigners.

Believe me, that is not adulation. I have known dozens of princes, but never one like the count.

For sheer grandeur, take his ambassadorship in Rome in 1628. The three cardinals, Sandoval, Espínola and Albornoz, a brother of the count of Elda, who later was viceroy of Sardinia, and a brother of the count of Távara, who became governor of Sicily, stayed with him. Each had his own apartment and his own guests, but the household was never for a moment disordered. There seemed to be an infinite number of chefs and butlers who could never be defeated—and the cutlery never ran out!

Every guest had a waiter and a valet given him, and there was always a carriage whenever anyone wanted one. The count ran his house of thirty-two rooms like that, summer and winter, without borrowing as much as a spoon from anyone.

The greatest celebration he ever gave was in October 1629, on the occasion of the birth of the royal prince—may God protect him. It was such a festa that even today the Romans and such foreigners as were in Rome at the time still talk about it. There was theater, jousting, fireworks, and fountains of wine. The count gave away alms to all the hospitals, and every evening for three days handfuls of gold and silver were thrown out into the streets of Rome. And though the Romans did not like us, when faced with such munificence and spectacle they all shouted, "Viva Espana!"

And who in Rome but the count had kept as many as four captains on full pay—thirty *escudos* a month—out of his own pocket and paid up regularly?

It was the count's treasurer Gaspar de Rosales who dealt with that sort of thing. He never gave anyone reason to grumble to his boss. Eventually, Gaspar de Rosales became secretary of state and of war at Naples when the count of Monterey became viceroy there. It certainly was well deserved. Gaspar de Rosales was a hardworking and honest man. I have often noticed that a man succeeds by having good servants and if he has misfortunes, it is because he has bad ones.

And then again, what viceroy has there ever been, who has taken so much trouble to seek out men of merit, who before he took them up, were stuck in some corner of a castle, without money and without recognition? I know plenty of cases.

What other viceroy has ever sent to Milan, in only fifteen months, two squadrons of Italian infantry of three thousand men each and as much as 700,000 ducats? And to Spain six thousand

infantry and a thousand horses in twenty-four galleons? The
infantry he sent to Spain under the command of the marquis of
Campo Lataro and the cavalry under the prince of La Rochela.
And as a special gift for his majesty, and his highness the infante
cardinal, the viceroy sent at the same time as the six thousand
infantry, twenty-four fine horses, with embroidered saddles and
bridles and on each horse's back a brocade coverlet reaching
nearly to the ground. Each, too, had pistols, which could not be
bought for any price, in the saddle holsters.

And as for madame the countess, she was a great lady. She
spent her days in the various hospitals for women, serving the
unfortunates with her own hands and bringing them food from
the palace. I have seen it and I know. She also founded a convent
for repentant Spanish women as well as maintaining many other
charities. She was a woman who never turned anyone away who
asked her to intercede for them.

I do not think I have exaggerated. On the contrary, I feel I have
said less than I might and I swear by this cross that at the time of
this writing, 4 February 1633, though I am in Palermo and in
disgrace, as I shall soon explain, despite my position I consider it
to be a greater honor to be their servant than to serve anyone else,
as I shall never be ungrateful for all their goodwill, and for all the
bread I have broken under their roof.

To return to my story about the parade in Naples on 20 June
1632. After the mock battle we went home worn out and sweat-
ing. The next day, I got orders to man the coastline with all the
cavalry we had. I had received news that a Turkish battle fleet was
in the offing. I led off five hundred horses to the principality of
Citra and took up positions between Eboli and Agropoli, where
we stayed until August of that same year, 1632.

Even in the dog days, it was so cold there that one had to sleep
under two blankets. And so, by day, we used to keep warm
skirmishing among ourselves and competing at picking up a ring
on the end of our lances.

† THE TALE OF THE VICIOUS HORSE †

In the company, there was a big four-year-old charger which was thoroughly vicious. He had already lamed four soldiers. To try to shoe him, we used to tie all his four legs, but once on the ground he would get so ferocious he would break the ropes however thick. So I gave orders that he was to be given as a present to the Franciscan monastery.

The guardian there said, "If the captain is giving us this horse as a present, would he also give us a contract proving it is a gift, so that we may sell it."

That night, the horse was so wild that no one even dared to go near enough to give it water to drink. The next day, I made out the contract and delivered it myself. When I got there, the guardian said to me, "Señor, I very much fear that this horse will kill one of the friars."

Then, he went off with the contract to the monastery. The next day, however, he came to me and said, "Señor, the horse is keeping quiet and seems to be much less fiery."

What happened was that within a week the horse became as tame as an old donkey, and he was harnessed up with a mare at the monastery and they worked side by side most happily and he forgot his masculine past. It was quite astonishing.

† HOW I DID NOT DIE †

I had another horse called Colona and one day when we were off for our tilting and horseplay, as we went every day to do in the mall by the Franciscan monastery, I mounted her. She was a good-tempered mare, and I had many times before played my games on her. But that day, she would not move an inch. I got angry and spurred her. She got under way for four paces, then stopped again. I turned her back and tried again, but she did not want to go anywhere very much, and if she had to go, she preferred to go sideways.

Some of my soldiers said, "Dismount, sir, she won't run today."

Then one of them added, "Give her to me, sir, I'll make her run and I'll break her of her little vices."

I dismounted and the soldier got on. Hardly was he in the saddle when the mare careered off straight toward a stone wall and hit it full tilt, killing both horse and rider. I was stricken with horror.

"What was it that had saved me? Was it the gift of the horse to the Franciscans? Was it the altar I had built to have masses said at for my soul in purgatory? Was it the fact that my altar was a privileged one, by order of the pope? God alone knows why I was not killed. I give thanks for this grace and for all the others which He grants me every day.

† I LEAVE NAPLES IN DISGRACE †

I returned to Naples with my company and we went into quarters by the Maddalena Bridge, from where every night I used to take out twenty horsemen and patrol south of Naples to Torre del Greco. The other companies did the same north of the town toward Pozzuoli.

I had very good horses in the company, but the men were not as good as their horses, so the count agreed with me that they should be disbanded and the company raised again. His excellency then made me the generous offer of the governorship of Pescara, one of the best jobs in the kingdom. I kissed his hand for the favor and waited in Naples patiently for a whole month for my orders.

Then one day his secretary, Rosales, came to tell me that the count wanted me to refit two little galleons and a fleet tender, which were in port, and go to the Levant to do a little piracy for him. At that time, my brother was with me. He had done twenty years military service in Italy and in the royal fleet. He had started as a soldier, risen to sergeant and sergeant major, and had spent three years on special service with eight *escudos* extra pay. At this time, he had just been discharged with the rank of lieutenant of heavy cavalry.

"Señor," I said to the count's secretary, "I will do what the count wants me to do, as long as the count provides for my brother. At least let him hold my post in Pescara until I return."

"Impossible," he replied, "There must be a captain for the post."

Then I asked him if I could see the count myself and ask him to give my brother the command of the fleet tender. But he would not agree. So next I suggested that my brother raise a company of the adventurers and flotsam of the waterfront and sail with me in that capacity. To that he agreed. Then I started to refit and store the ships. But when it was half done, I said to the secretary, "Don't make a monkey of me or I won't sail on this expedition. I swear by God I won't if this business is not settled. Tell the count what I say."

No word was heard, until one night when the secretary came to me and said, "The count will not give your brother any commission, but you are both to sail on this cruise together."

I went home to think things out. I had no post in Naples and no pay from the king (nor had my brother), despite the fact that my brother had said to the count, "I have served well as everyone knows and your grace has helped many men, but I have been unable to get any promotion and the world will think that I am no good."

And he was quite justified in what he said. So I collected together my belongings and went to stay at the monastery of the Most Holy Trinity.

There, I wrote a letter to the secretary, which read something like this, "You may be surprised that I have been so insistent on my brother being given a post, but if I went on your expedition and died, my brother would be the only one left as head of a family of orphans and nephews and nieces. You have taken away my last hope this evening and I have therefore decided to refuse the count's orders. You may tell the count that I have retired to this monastery to reconsider how to make a living and, of course, in the fear that his excellency might out of fury throw me into the castle dungeons. I am willing to carry out his orders even now provided my brother is made captain. He deserves it, and the count has in any case already promised it once. Then I will come out of this monastery and go to sea and do my duty well."

The secretary was shocked when he realized that I was not going to do as I was told. He wrote me a wheedling letter, but I firmly answered that I would not move an inch without his agreement to my conditions.

I then asked the count for leave for myself, my brother, and my nephew to quit Naples, to which he replied, "A ticket of leave is quite unnecessary. You are a knight of Malta, and not in the pay or employ of this kingdom. All you need is a bill of health."

I sent word back saying, "I am not the sort of man who leaves a place where he has been employed without at least a letter giving me permission to go. And if your excellency will not give me one I shall stay here until I die or until your excellency is promoted to a higher command."

Only then did the count dictate and sign with his own hand excellent references giving us permission to go, me to Malta, my brother to Spain, and my nephew to Sicily. They were all sent to me at the monastery.

Next day, I received a letter from the secretary, but it came from much higher quarters really, asking me to write some instructions on what the ships should do when they got to the Levant. While the messenger waited, I wrote out a detailed instruction, adding at the end, "Sir, I am no angel, and I can err. The navigator's advice should be asked, and if it seems to be a good plan, follow it; if not, don't. What I have written is what I myself intended to do had I not the ill luck to have brothers."

Shortly thereafter, I packed my bags, though everyone, even the palace ministers, said to me, "Wait a little."

I decided against their advice but called to see Secretary Rosales, with whom I spent a long time. He told me that I had made a grave error. We agreed to meet the next evening, but I could see no good coming from it. In fact I feared the opposite. At midnight, then, I went aboard a felucca with my brother and my nephew with such goods as I possessed, and we sailed from Naples that night, 20 December.

I forgot to tell you that my retreat into the monastery started a rumor that I had become a monk. This was, of course, impossible, as I had already taken my vows in the Order of St. John. It was even in the *Gazette,* and I got a letter from Malta saying that news had reached there that I was a Capuchin. It was not surprising that such a story got abroad, as there were some people in Naples who swore they had seen me celebrating mass. They did not know that I did not understand a word of Latin.

However, I passed a penitential two months in that monastery, with four masses in the morning, and vespers in the evening, and for lunch and dinner a chicken and excellent old wine and everything that went with it.

† PLEASANT VOYAGE TO PALERMO †

It was a rough night when we left Naples, but at dawn we found ourselves off Vietri—sixty miles from Naples. We crossed the Gulf of Salerno and rounded Cape Palinuro. We were not allowed ashore there because of some epidemic. We sailed on to Paola, where I stayed two days, visiting the birthplace of St. Francis of Paola. From there, we went on south to Pizzo, where we met a felucca bound for Naples. Aboard her was a young Spanish lady whom I knew. She said she was frightened of being alone, so we dined that night together. She also asked me to sleep in her room. I did so, but of course in another bed.

During the night, I got up to make water, and, while I was feeling my way back to my bed in the dark, I slipped and fell into the Spanish lady's bed. She pretended to be asleep, but she was wide awake and very beautiful. I took my opportunity, and she, all the time, pretended to be asleep. When it was over, she woke up and said, "What have you done?"

"Touch there and you will soon find out," I said.

She did so and said, "What a wicked old man you are, by Jesus!"

"Yes, no doubt," I replied, "and I am sure you would have preferred a younger man to look at in the morning."

But for all that, even though I am an old man, I met her thrust for thrust and, by God, she was worth the trouble.

In the morning, we watered the feluccas and our ships parted company. That evening, we reached Tropea, but I did not stay the night there, as I wanted to get to Messina for Christmas Eve.

We spent Christmas at an inn in Messina. There was a deal of woman flesh there, but since it was a vigil, we all kept quiet, me especially, as I had had my oats.

We heard mass, in fact several masses, and then sailed. But as we could not manage to double the lighthouse cape, we slept that night in Messina.

We again took to the sea and struggled on as far as Milazzo, where we stayed that night and the next day as well because of bad weather. The captain at arms there made me a present of chickens, wine, and a goat, which filled up my store cupboard. We had a party at an inn, where there was no shortage of either boy or girl devils.

We left Milazzo and without touching land got as far as Termini, where we found excellent lodgings. We slept there and sailed in the morning. At midday, we reached Palermo.

I found dozens of old friends, and so I decided to set up house there. But before I did anything about it, I went to see the duke of Alcalá, the viceroy of the kingdom of Sicily.

I informed him of my arrival, which he knew about already, and asked him for the thirty *escudos* pay that was owing to me. He gave orders that I was to be paid at once.

My brother submitted a memorandum asking his excellency, in consideration of his services, for a captaincy and the right to raise a company. There were not many troops in Sicily at that time. I offered to put up five hundred ducats, which was the usual sum paid to a captain for his expenses in raising a company, and so save the viceroy the expense, but the reply was that there would have to be an inquiry into what should be done.

This ended in my brother being recommended to go to Flanders and being put on a Catalan ship, loaded with biscuits and bound for Genoa. I gave him two hundred golden *escudos* and clothes, and I paid for his passage and food. I gave him my blessing and said, "Go to Flanders, my boy, and you will get a captaincy there. You have done good service. You are well equipped, you have a letter of recommendation and money in your pocket. May God be with you."

So in God's keeping he sailed. I stayed here until today, 4 February 1633, when I am writing this. If God grants me longer life and if anything of interest happens, I shall add it to this story.

CHAPTER EIGHTEEN

It was in 1633 that my brother went to Flanders, as I have described, and I stayed on in Palermo. His excellency the duke of Alcalá, viceroy of Sicily, sent for me. I went to the palace, and he said, "What has been happening between you and Monterey?"

"Nothing," I replied. "He has given me leave to go to Malta."

He pressed me with questions, but I would not tell him anything of what had happened at Naples. At the end of the interview, I went down to the palace guardroom. There the captains badgered me immediately to find out the news.

"Now leave the count alone," I said, "he may be nearly a dwarf, but he is the greatest grandee of the lot."

That was soon reported to the duke, who was very annoyed. He had his secretary call me and say, "Pay Don Jerónimo de Castro the two hundred *escudos* you owe him."

This Jerónimo de Castro was in the room at the time, and I said to the secretary, "Señor, it is perfectly true that this gentleman gave me two hundred *escudos*. He gave them to me to get a papal brief that he wanted to submit to the grand master. The fact that the grand master would not accept it was no fault of mine. I fulfilled my part of the bargain in getting the brief."

"That is no excuse," replied the secretary. "I want the money here in an hour or you will be thrown into prison."

Seeing that he meant what he said, I replied, "Very well, send someone with me to carry this money and I will be back within the hour."

I went off under guard, and the money was brought back in a little bag. I handed it to the secretary, saying, "There you are. Give the money to the viceroy for any little whim he needs to satisfy, but not to Don Jerónimo de Castro."

Then I went back to my lodging pondering the ways of the world. Two days later, I received a visit from a sergeant major, who announced to me, "His excellency desires to settle his accounts with you and the rights you say you have to payment here."

"I have no pay here," I replied. "I have a ticket of leave from the count of Monterey, and I am on my way to Malta." After that brush, I decided to see the collector of the Order of St. John of Jerusalem, and he spoke to the viceroy on my behalf and I was at last left alone.

After twenty days, I received letters and certificates from the Order in Malta, settling on me the estates and commandery of San Juan de Puente de Orbi. After two more months in Palermo, I found two Genoese galleys that were going to Spain, carrying a bishop, so I said to the captain, "I will come with you through Naples, provided you don't tell the count of Monterey."

He agreed immediately to my condition, but the first thing he did was to send the count word that I was aboard. The count already knew by the *Gazettes* that I had been in Sicily.

Secretary Rosales then sent aboard a curt note, saying, "The count knows you are here. Come to dinner as I have a few words to say to you."

I could not dodge it, so I went ashore to the palace where I met Rosales. I showed him the certificates that gave me my commandery in Spain. He was astonished and rushed up to tell the count.

When the count heard the news, he said, "He has got something there which stops me being angry with him anymore. Find out more about it, by God, and make him stay with us here."

We dined, and they talked and talked at me so that I had to stay on. The two galleys went on to Gaeta, where they were to join up with some others and were to sail in company with them to Genoa.

The secretary gave me a letter from the count to deliver to the marchioness of Charela at Gaeta, which I did. The next day, when the cannon fired for the departure of the assembled galleys, the governor of Gaeta sent out an armed brigantine to take me aboard and back to Naples. But as my luggage was at the bottom of the hold and could not possibly be gotten out, I was able to refuse politely.

We made a good trip to Genoa, from where I went on home to Spain after a short stay.

† THE COURT AT MADRID †

In a few days, we were in Barcelona and from there I went to Madrid. I stayed with secretary Juan Ruiz de Contreras, who was father of Don Fernando, who is today so important in the government. He entertained me regally, and I set out staking my claims. The first thing I did was to take possession of my commandery.

On my return from León, where the commandery was, I met my brother, who was looking for a job and asking for the money still due to him when he was discharged in Flanders.

The council saw the justness of his case and gave him two hundred *escudos* and a letter of recommendation to Secretary Rojas telling him to give my brother a company. Rojas, in turn, wrote a letter to Secretary Pedro de Arce telling him of the council's wishes. Pedro de Arce appealed against it and dragged the affair out as long as he could, saying to the councillors of state that if I had been a cavalry captain it must have been a very strange cavalry squadron I had had. He could not believe me, and therefore my brother could not have his promotion.

I heard all about this after a few days and this is how. As my brother seemed to be waiting a long time for his commission to come through, I went to see the marquis of Santa Cruz, who was a member of the Council of State. I pressed him hard for an explanation, and at last he said, "How can you expect us to give your brother a company? Pedro de Arce tells us that if you were a cavalry captain, the post must have been come by dishonestly."

I turned on my heel without saying a word and went home, not even bothering to have my dinner. I got out my cavalry captain's commission, which showed that I had had a squadron of five hundred men, my discharge, and my ticket of leave and went back to see the marquis as fast as I could. I was announced and said, "I beg your excellency to hear me out. Twenty years ago, by the postern gate of San Martin, a certain lady called me. It was in the dead of night. I went up to her apartment, and we quickly found a topic of conversation to chat about. Then there was a knock at the door.

" 'Hide yourself,' she said. 'It is Pedro de Arce, but he won't stay long.'

" 'I'm not hiding for anybody,' I said. 'Let him in.'

"The woman, although she was afraid, gave orders for the door to be opened. Then up the stairs came Pedro with his sword and shield, looking as green as a lettuce. He was, at that time, serving in the Council of War. When he saw me, he asked, 'What are you doing here?'

" 'This lady is asking me some news of a friend of hers,' I replied.

"But before I could finish, he protected himself with his buckler and drew his sword. I got on my guard, too, and gave him such a wallop that he fell down the stairs—sword, shield, and all—shrieking, 'You've killed me!'

"However, he was not even wounded. I took advantage of the

ensuing riot to go my way with the grace of God. He was carried off to his lodgings half-dead from the fall. And since then he has always looked on me with a jaundiced eye. So, if your excellency will now look at this commission, this discharge, and this ticket of leave, he will be convinced that Pedro de Arce was lying out of sheer spite. I was a cavalry captain for seven months and three days."